12707

NIGERIA

NIGERIA

1880 TO THE PRESENT:
THE STRUGGLE, THE TRAGEDY, THE PROMISE

DANIEL E. HARMON

INTRODUCTORY ESSAY BY
Dr. Richard E. Leakey
Chairman, Wildlife Clubs
of Kenya Association
✝
AFTERWORD BY
Deirdre Shields

CHELSEA HOUSE PUBLISHERS
Philadelphia
In association with Covos Day Books, South Africa

CHELSEA HOUSE PUBLISHERS

EDITOR IN CHIEF Stephen Reginald
PRODUCTION MANAGER Pamela Loos
ART DIRECTOR Sara Davis
PICTURE EDITOR Judy L. Hasday
MANAGING EDITOR James D. Gallagher
SENIOR PRODUCTION EDITOR LeeAnne Gelletly
ASSOCIATE ART DIRECTOR Takeshi Takahashi
SERIES DESIGNER Keith Trego
COVER DESIGN Emiliano Begnardi

© 2001 by Chelsea House Publishers, a subsidiary of Haights Cross Communications. All rights reserved. Printed and bound in the United States of America.
The Chelsea House World Wide Web address is http://www.chelseahouse.com

3 5 7 9 8 6 4 2

Library of Congress Cataloging-in-Publication Data

Harmon, Daniel.
    Nigeria / Daniel Harmon.
        p. cm. — (Exploration of Africa, the emerging nations)
    Includes bibliographical references and index.
    Summary: Photographs and text look at the past, development, and present
culture of Nigeria and its inhabitants.
    ISBN 0-7910-5452-7
    1. Nigeria—History—Juvenile literature. [1. Nigeria.] I. Title.
    II. Series.
    DT515.58 .H37 2000
    966.9—dc21
                                                    99-058749

The photographs in this book are from the Royal Geographical Society Picture Library. Most are being published for the first time.

The Royal Geographical Society Picture Library provides an unrivaled source of over half a million images of peoples and landscapes from around the globe. Photographs date from the 1840s onwards on a variety of subjects including the British Colonial Empire, deserts, exploration, indigenous peoples, landscapes, remote destinations, and travel.

Photography, beginning with the daguerreotype in 1839, is only marginally younger than the Society, which encouraged its explorers to use the new medium from its earliest days. From the remarkable mid-19th century black-and-white photographs to color transparencies of the late 20th century, the focus of the collection is not the generic stock shot but the portrayal of man's resilience, adaptability and mobility in remote parts of the world.

In organizing this project, we have incurred many debts of gratitude. Our first, though, is to the professional staff of the Picture Library for their generous assistance, especially to Joanna Scadden, Picture Library Manager.

CONTENTS

Exploration of Africa: The Emerging Nations

THE DARK CONTINENT

DR. RICHARD E. LEAKEY

THE CONCEPT OF AFRICAN exploration has been greatly influenced by the hero status given to the European adventurers and missionaries who went off to Africa in the last century. Their travels and travails were certainly extraordinary and nobody can help but be impressed by the tremendous physical and intellectual courage that was so much a characteristic of people such as Livingstone, Stanley, Speke, and Baker, to name just a few. The challenges and rewards that Africa offered, both in terms of commerce and also "saved souls," inspired people to take incredible risks and endure personal suffering to a degree that was probably unique to the exploration of Africa.

I myself was fortunate enough to have had the opportunity to organize one or two minor expeditions to remote spots in Africa where there were no roads or airfields and marching with porters and/or camels was the best option at the time. I have also had the thrill of being with people untouched and often unmoved by contact with Western or other technologically based cultures, and these experiences remain for me amongst the most exciting and salutary of my life. With the contemporary revolution in technology, there will be few if any such opportunities again. Indeed I often find myself slightly saddened by the realization that were life ever discovered on another planet, exploration would doubtless be done by remote sensing and making full use of artificial, digital intelligence. At least it is unlikely to be in my lifetime and this is a relief!

INTRODUCTION

Notwithstanding all of this, I believe that the age of exploration and discovery in Africa is far from over. The future offers incredible opportunities for new discoveries that will push back the frontiers of knowledge. This endeavor will of course not involve exotic and arduous journeys into malaria-infested tropical swamps, but it will certainly require dedication, team work, public support, and a conviction that the rewards to be gained will more than justify the efforts and investment.

EARLY EXPLORERS

Many of us were raised and educated at school with the belief that Africa, the so-called Dark Continent, was actually discovered by early European travelers and explorers. The date of this "discovery" is difficult to establish, and anyway a distinction has always had to be drawn between northern Africa and the vast area south of the Sahara. The Romans certainly had information about the continent's interior as did others such as the Greeks. A diverse range of traders ventured down both the west coast and the east coast from at least the ninth century, and by the tenth century Islam had taken root in a number of new towns and settlements established by Persian and Arab interests along the eastern tropical shores. Trans-African trade was probably under way well before this time, perhaps partly stimulated by external interests.

Close to the beginning of the first millennium, early Christians were establishing the Coptic church in the ancient kingdom of Ethiopia and at other coastal settlements along Africa's northern Mediterranean coast. Along the west coast of Africa, European trade in gold, ivory, and people was well established by the sixteenth century. Several hundred years later, early in the 19th century, the systematic penetration and geographical exploration of Africa was undertaken by Europeans seeking geographical knowledge and territory and looking for opportunities not only for commerce but for the chance to spread the Gospel. The extraordinary narratives of some of the journeys of early European travelers and adventurers in Africa are a vivid reminder of just how recently Africa has become embroiled in the power struggles and vested interests of non-Africans.

THE DARK CONTINENT

AFRICA'S GIFT TO THE WORLD

My own preoccupation over the past thirty years has been to study human prehistory, and from this perspective it is very clear that Africa was never "discovered" in the sense in which so many people have been and, perhaps, still are being taught. Rather, it was Africans themselves who found that there was a world beyond their shores.

Prior to about two million years ago, the only humans or proto-humans in existence were confined to Africa; as yet, the remaining world had not been exposed to this strange mammalian species, which in time came to dominate the entire planet. It is no trivial matter to recognize the cultural implications that arise from this entirely different perspective of Africa and its relationship to the rest of humanity.

How many of the world's population grow up knowing that it was in fact African people who first moved and settled in southern Europe and Central Asia and migrated to the Far East? How many know that Africa's principal contribution to the world is in fact humanity itself? These concepts are quite different from the notion that Africa was only "discovered" in the past few hundred years and will surely change the commonly held idea that somehow Africa is a "laggard," late to come onto the world stage.

It could be argued that our early human forebears—the *Homo erectus* who moved out of Africa—have little or no bearing on the contemporary world and its problems. I disagree and believe that the often pejorative thoughts that are associated with the Dark Continent and dark skins, as well as with the general sense that Africans are somehow outside the mainstream of human achievement, would be entirely negated by the full acceptance of a universal African heritage for all of humanity. This, after all, is the truth that has now been firmly established by scientific inquiry.

The study of human origins and prehistory will surely continue to be important in a number of regions of Africa and this research must continue to rank high on the list of relevant ongoing exploration and discovery. There is still much to be learned about the early stages of human development, and the age of the "first humans"—the first bipedal apes—has not been firmly established. The current hypothesis is that prior to five million years ago there were no bipeds, and this would mean that humankind is only five million years old. Beyond Africa, there were no humans until just two million years ago, and this is a consideration that political leaders and people as a whole need to bear in mind.

RECENT HISTORY

When it comes to the relatively recent history of Africa's contemporary people, there is still considerable ignorance. The evidence suggests that there were major migrations of people within the continent during the past 5,000 years, and the impact of the introduction of domestic stock must have been quite considerable on the way of life of many of Africa's people. Early settlements and the beginnings of nation states are, as yet, poorly researched and recorded. Although archaeological studies have been undertaken in Africa for well over a hundred years, there remain more questions than answers.

One question of universal interest concerns the origin and inspiration for the civilization of early Egypt. The Nile has, of course, offered opportunities for contacts between the heart of Africa and the Mediterranean seacoast, but very little is known about human settlement and civilization in the upper reaches of the Blue and White Nile between 4,000 and 10,000 years ago. We do know that the present Sahara Desert is only about 10,000 years old; before this Central Africa was wetter and more fertile, and research findings have shown that it was only during the past 10,000 years that Lake Turkana in the northern Kenya was isolated from the Nile system. When connected, it would have been an excellent connection between the heartland of the continent and the Mediterranean.

Another question focuses on the extensive stone-walled villages and towns in Southern Africa. The Great Zimbabwe is but one of thousands of standing monuments in East, Central, and Southern Africa that attest to considerable human endeavor in Africa long before contact with Europe or Arabia. The Neolithic period and Iron Age still offer very great opportunities for exploration and discovery.

As an example of the importance of history, let us look at the modern South Africa where a visitor might still be struck by the not-too-subtle representation of a past that, until a few years ago, only "began" with the arrival of Dutch settlers some 400 years back. There are, of course, many pre-Dutch sites, including extensive fortified towns where kingdoms and nation states had thrived hundreds of years before contact with Europe; but this evidence has been poorly documented and even more poorly portrayed.

Few need to be reminded of the sparseness of Africa's precolonial written history. There are countless cultures and historical narratives that have been recorded only as oral history and legend. As postcolonial Africa further consolidates itself, history must be reviewed and deepened to incorporate the realities of precolonial human settlement as well as foreign contact. Africa's identity and self-respect is closely linked to this.

One of the great tragedies is that African history was of little interest to the early European travelers who were in a hurry and had no brief to document the details of the people they came across during their travels. In the basements of countless European museums, there are stacked shelves of African "curios"—objects taken from the people but seldom documented in terms of the objects' use, customs, and history.

There is surely an opportunity here for contemporary scholars to do something. While much of Africa's precolonial past has been obscured by the slave trade, colonialism, evangelism, and modernization, there remains an opportunity, at least in some parts of the continent, to record what still exists. This has to be one of the most vital frontiers for African exploration and discovery as we approach the end of this millennium. Some of the work will require trips to the field, but great gains could be achieved by a systematic and coordinated effort to record the inventories of European museums and archives. The Royal Geographical Society could well play a leading role in this chapter of African exploration. The compilation of a central data bank on what is known and what exists would, if based on a coordinated initiative to record the customs and social organization of Africa's remaining indigenous peoples, be a huge contribution to the heritage of humankind.

MEDICINES AND FOODS

On the African continent itself, there remain countless other areas for exploration and discovery. Such endeavors will be achieved without the fanfare of great expeditions and high adventure as was the case during the last century and they should, as far as possible, involve exploration and discovery of African frontiers by Africans themselves. These frontiers are not geographic: they are boundaries of knowledge in the sphere of Africa's home-grown cultures and natural world.

Indigenous knowledge is a very poorly documented subject in many parts of the world, and Africa is a prime example of a continent where centuries of accumulated local knowledge is rapidly disappearing in the face of modernization. I believe, for example, that there is much to be learned about the use of wild African plants for both medicinal and nutritional purposes. Such knowledge, kept to a large extent as the experience and memory of elders in various indigenous communities, could potentially have far-reaching benefits for Africa and for humanity as a whole.

The importance of new remedies based on age-old medicines cannot be underestimated. Over the past two decades, international companies have begun to take note and to exploit certain African plants for pharmacological preparations. All too often, Africa has not been the beneficiary of these "discoveries," which are, in most instances, nothing more than the refinement and improvement of traditional African medicine. The opportunities for exploration and discovery in this area are immense and will have assured economic return on investment. One can only hope that such work will be in partnership with the people of Africa and not at the expense of the continent's best interests.

Within the same context, there is much to be learned about the traditional knowledge of the thousands of plants that have been utilized by different African communities for food. The contemporary world has become almost entirely dependent, in terms of staple foods, on the cultivation of only six principal plants: corn, wheat, rice, yams, potatoes, and bananas. This cannot be a secure basis to guarantee the food requirements of more than five billion people.

Many traditional food plants in Africa are drought resistant and might well offer new alternatives for large-scale agricultural development in the years to come. Crucial to this development is finding out what African people used before exotics were introduced. In some rural areas of the continent, it is still possible to learn about much of this by talking to the older generation. It is certainly a great shame that some of the early European travelers in Africa were ill equipped to study and record details of diet and traditional plant use, but I am sure that, although it is late, it is not too late. The compilation of a pan-African database on what is known about the use of the continent's plant resources is a vital matter requiring action.

VANISHING SPECIES

In the same spirit, there is as yet a very incomplete inventory of the continent's other species. The inevitable trend of bringing land into productive management is resulting in the loss of unknown but undoubtedly large numbers of species. This genetic resource may be invaluable to the future of Africa and indeed humankind, and there really is a need for coordinated efforts to record and understand the continent's biodiversity.

In recent years important advances have been made in the study of tropical ecosystems in Central and South America, and I am sure that similar endeavors in Africa would be rewarding. At present, Africa's semi-arid and highland ecosystems are better understood than the more diverse and complex lowland forests, which are themselves under particular threat from loggers and farmers. The challenges of exploring the biodiversity of the upper canopy in the tropical forests, using the same techniques that are now used in Central American forests, are fantastic and might also lead to eco-tourist developments for these areas in the future.

It is indeed an irony that huge amounts of money are being spent by the advanced nations in an effort to discover life beyond our own planet, while at the same time nobody on this planet knows the extent and variety of life here at home. The tropics are especially relevant in this regard and one can only hope that Africa will become the focus of renewed efforts of research on biodiversity and tropical ecology.

AN AFROCENTRIC VIEW

Overall, the history of Africa has been presented from an entirely Eurocentric or even Caucasocentric perspective, and until recently this has not been adequately reviewed. The penetration of Africa, especially during the last century, was important in its own way; but today the realities of African history, art, culture, and politics are better known. The time has come to regard African history in terms of what has happened in Africa itself, rather than simply in terms of what non-African individuals did when they first traveled to the continent.

Ceramic Figures in an Arochuku House, Southern Nigeria, 1925 *The town of Arochuku in southern Nigeria, called Juju by the British, was the center of the Aro people, an Ibo subgroup that dominated southern Nigeria politically in the eighteenth and nineteenth centuries. Local artisans are still noted for their metalwork and carving skills. Arochuku is now a market center and the site of a teacher-training college.*

INTRODUCTION

In the late 1800s Europeans nicknamed Prince Otto von Bismarck the "Iron Chancellor." As ruler of Prussia and later of the united German Empire, he was probably the most feared—and most disliked—national leader in Europe. He had a habit of casually nibbling fruit and shellfish while conferring with foreign leaders and ambassadors. His intentions, they all knew, however, were anything but casual. He was a cold, calculating player in the game of power; one who was never to be completely trusted.

A tall, daring man, Bismarck entered politics during the 1840s and eventually rose to Prussia's highest imperial office. Prussia at the time was a large kingdom spreading south from the North Sea and the Baltic Sea. Bismarck's early vision was to unite Prussia with the other ancient German states to the south.

This he did—by force. From 1864 to 1870 he deliberately provoked wars with three neighboring countries (Denmark, Austria, and France) in order to gain certain border provinces he wanted to include in his unified Germany. Bismarck's military leadership was ingenious. With "blood and iron," as observers of his day remarked, he acquired the territories he coveted and forged his enormous empire.

In late 1884 Bismarck called a meeting of representatives from all the major European governments. Special emissaries were dispatched to Berlin to join their countries' ambassadors. Speculation was high. No one knew exactly what the Iron Chancellor wanted to talk about, but they knew their nations had better be represented. They also knew it had something to do with Africa.

A Continent Becomes a Chessboard

What did this gigantic foreign continent, awkwardly straddling the equator with an unnerving mixture of endless desert and fever-plagued jungle, have to do with refined European politics? We examine the reasons in detail later. For now the short answer is that by controlling the richest parts of Africa, European nations could make themselves stronger and more influential in the chess game of international politics. Or so they believed.

For many years European countries had been jockeying to control the trading systems along the African coast, although few whites had ventured very far into the continent's interior. Of the 14 nations represented at Bismarck's conference, the most prominent ones were England, France, and Portugal—all three long established in the African coastal trade—and two relative newcomers, Belgium and Germany.

The conference hall was, interestingly, the broad music room of Bismarck's home. A huge chandelier hung from the center of the high ceiling. Regal carpet and drapes gave the chamber a solemn, stately appearance. Representatives from the great nations sat around tables, presided over by Bismarck himself. Outside, the streets of Berlin were cold and messy with the slush of melting snow.

As the host, Bismarck gave the opening address on Saturday afternoon, November 15, 1884. The ambassadors were eager to hear what he had to say—and to speculate on what he avoided saying—about German interests in the so-called Dark Continent. What would become known as the West Africa Conference had begun.

Bismarck's viewpoint—at least his *stated* viewpoint—was that Europe should not try to *rule* Africa, but to *help* it. The European nations, he explained, were morally obligated to bring Africa in line with the rest of civilization. As part of the effort to "help" this strange, little-known continent, Bismarck reasoned, increased

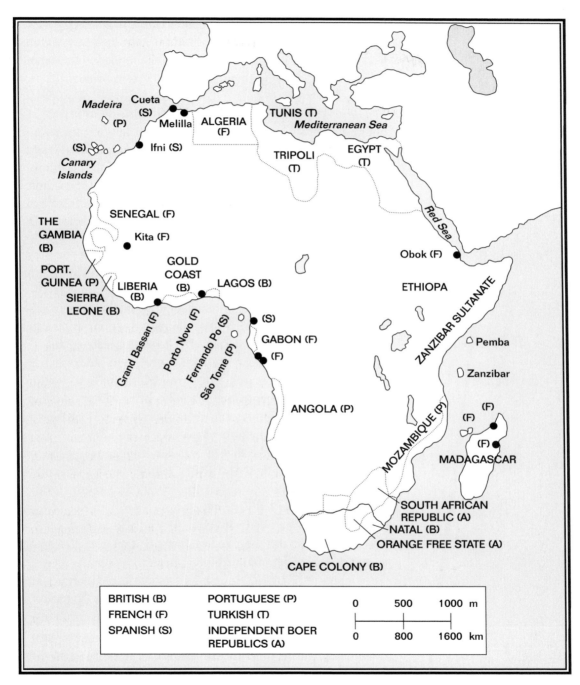

Africa on the Eve of Partition, Showing Extent of Conquest by 1880.

**Exterior of the Harem,
Emir of Kano's Palace,
c. 1900** *In Muslim countries,
a harem was that part of a
house set aside for the
women of the family.*

European trade would greatly benefit the Africans. (The fact that the crafty European-African trade agreements promised to help European businesses far more than they would the African tribes must have seemed hardly worth mentioning, to Bismarck.) Humanity and peace for Africa were Bismarck's stated goals.

British ambassador Sir Edward Malet, who addressed the conference after Bismarck, also stressed the natives' welfare. Britain at that time controlled the Niger River. Everyone knew Malet's underlying interest at the conference was preserving this valuable river domain for England.

England was worried that the other European nations would try to "internationalize" the Niger region. Britain especially feared the expanding power of France, its archenemy. France had already beaten out rival nations in controlling the Senegal region on the West African coast. If England were forced to loosen its grip on the Niger region at the conference, then Malet would insist on "internationalizing" Senegal as well.

Bismarck confirmed England's fears in his opening statement. Among other objectives, he proposed that the Niger River be open for boats of all countries to navigate. (Not surprisingly, Germany was closely allied to France at that point in history.)

Actually, however, the Berlin conference was not as concerned about either the Niger or Senegal territories as it was about the Congo, some five hundred miles from the Niger River basin in south central Africa. Though less populated, the Congo was much larger than the Niger and Senegal territories combined. Henry Morton Stanley, one of the most famous explorers of Africa, believed that although the Congo was landlocked, for trade purposes it should be expanded. He proposed a "geographic and commercial Congo basin" that spanned south central Africa from the Indian Ocean across to the Atlantic Ocean.

These were the kinds of international politics at stake in Berlin. Besides the formal discussions in the conference chamber, delegates conferred quietly among themselves in the corridors and offices of nearby buildings.

The conference ended in February 1885 with the signing of the Act of Berlin. Delegates insisted they had not "partitioned" Africa; they had merely set forth orderly trade domains and procedures. The European powers agreed that a nation's claims over African territory would be accepted on only two conditions:

1. The nation making the claim had to officially notify the other nations of its claim.

2. It had to demonstrate that it actually held authority in the region.

Several humanitarian gestures were also made. The European leaders formally opposed slavery (endorsing the stance England had championed for more than half a century) and pledged to protect Christian missions. They also considered banning the sale of liquor to African natives, but Bismarck personally opposed that clause. (Perhaps he did so because the Iron Chancellor owned several distilleries, and liquor made up more than half of Germany's exports to West Africa!) As a result of his persuasion, the wording of the Berlin agreement was altered to state that liquor would be regulated but not banned.

Why Africa?

To return to our question: Why did the European powers feel a need to control Africa? The answer was partly because it was so vast and seemed so available. At least, it looked easily available

A Walled Egba Village, Near Abeokuta, Southwestern Nigeria, c. 1883 *Modern Abeokuta is situated on the east bank of the Ogun River 48 miles north of Lagos. It is a major exporting point for cocoa, palm oil, fruits, and kola nuts. Cotton weaving and dyeing with locally grown indigo are the traditional crafts of the town. Population (2000 est.) 440,000.*

on a map or a globe, to wealthy leaders like Bismarck, who had no desire to go there in person. Bismarck once remarked that "my map of Africa lies in Europe. Here is Russia, and here lies France, and we are in the middle."

Throughout modern history, nations have clamored to control the earth's lands and seas. For three centuries following Columbus, European powers fought each other to possess different regions of the Americas. They had little regard for the rights of the many Native American tribes who already lived there. Europe's new colonies overseas sent wealth back to the home countries.

Africa had been discovered by the Europeans much earlier than had America. The first white visitors to Africa, however, quickly learned the dangers and difficulties of trying to establish control. As late as the 1870s, European countries "controlled" only 10 percent of the continent. Their settlements were coastal colonies, many of which had been established by slave traders.

Suddenly, however, leaders not only in Europe but in countries like the United States and Japan became interested in Africa. It seemed to be just waiting for them to claim.

The Europeans had mixed reasons for wanting a share of Africa. In Egypt, at the northeastern corner of the continent, for example, the English realized it was possible to connect the

Mediterranean Sea with the Indian Ocean via a canal. Such a shortcut would take weeks off the ocean passage for every ship traveling between England and India. Until the Suez Canal opened, vessels had been forced to sail the entire length of Africa's Atlantic coast and around the Cape of Good Hope.

Other countries hoped to find riches in the African interior. Europeans operated diamond mines in South Africa long before the Berlin conference. Indeed, some historians hold that profit was the main reason behind all European and American relations with Africa for centuries.

Many church denominations saw the "primitive" continent as a vast mission field. Some people outside the church believed it their duty not necessarily to convert African natives to Christianity but to "civilize" the tribes and improve the poor living conditions. They shuddered at reports of life in the wild, where housing and water were, by European standards, grossly unsanitary. In Africa the infant death rate was high and the average life expectancy short. The tribal systems of justice and punishment seemed brutal to refined Europeans, who found the age-old customs grotesque and incomprehensible.

At least one country, Italy, wanted to establish colonies across the Mediterranean to help relieve the growing population inside its own country.

All the while, there was the matter of influence. The more territory a nation controlled, the more formidable it appeared to rival nations.

The Scramble

Many writers have termed the West African Conference a carving up of Africa by the European leaders. The result, they said, was a scramble for control of the continent.

Actually, as historian Thomas Pakenham has pointed out, the scramble for Africa began years before Bismarck's conference. When all was said and done, the agreement drawn up in Berlin was lengthy but not especially significant. "It had set no rules for dividing, let alone eating, the cake," Pakenham wrote.

**Africa Before the Scramble:
Indigenous and Alien
Powers in 1876**

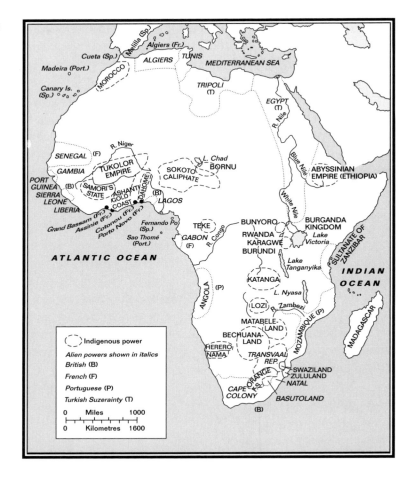

Certainly, though, what happened after the Berlin conference could be described as a scramble. By 1900 the European nations had divided Africa into approximately forty political units and claimed control over all but six of them.

The Europeans soon discovered, however, that *claiming* Africa and *controlling* what they had claimed were two very different matters. Africa was an enormous unknown. As they pressed inward from the coast, white explorers each day discovered different terrain, different tribes with different customs and beliefs, different sets of hardships and requirements for sur-

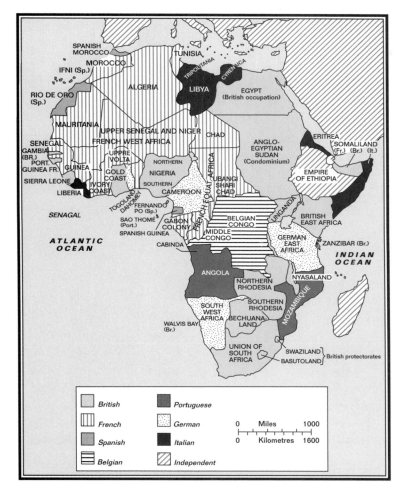

Africa after the Scramble, 1912

vival. They gradually uncovered a continent with many peoples and kingdoms far more complex than their own. These kingdoms often fought among themselves for reasons the visitors did not fully understand. To make matters even more confusing, everything was constantly changing.

Woman Spinning Cotton, 1908 *Cotton spinning was a traditional industry of those living along the banks of the Niger River. In 1906 the British chose the west central town of Baro, originally a small Nupe village, as a link between rail and river transportation. Its solid riverbank, rare along the Niger River, could be used for unloading boats carrying northern Nigerian cotton onto trains.*

What Brought Europeans to Nigeria?

T he Federal Republic of Nigeria is found just north of the equator in the elbow of West Africa, on the southern coast of the continent's great bulge into the Atlantic Ocean. Encompassing 356,669 square miles (slightly smaller than the State of Montana), it is by no means Africa's largest nation, geographically. Nevertheless, it has the most people of all the African countries: more than 120 million residents, according to recent estimates. In the words of John de St. Jorre, who covered the 1967–1970 Biafran war for the London *Observer* and later wrote a book about it, "Nigeria is truly the giant of Africa."

Nigeria today is flanked by the Sahara Desert nation of Niger on the north, Cameroon and Chad on the east, and Benin on the west. The southern edge of the country is seacoast, at the Gulf of Guinea (Atlantic Ocean).

Nigeria's capital, Abuja, is a relatively new city in the center of the country, about 100 miles from the fork of the Niger River and its largest tributary, the Benue (or Binue). The country's most important port, Lagos, is also the country's largest city in terms of population. Once the Nigerian capital, Lagos is located on the southwestern coast, near the Benin border.

When did the Europeans "discover" Africa? It's an interesting question—especially to native Africans who well might ask, instead, when *they* discovered the *Europeans*.

The Mediterranean coast in the north has been familiar to non-African civilizations for thousands of years. Historical records suggest that the Romans 2,000 years ago and the Greeks before them knew something of the continent's interior. By the end of the first millennium A.D., European and Middle Eastern traders were operating along the African coasts in both the Atlantic and Indian oceans. The Islamic religion by that time had been introduced by the Middle Easterns at settlements along the continent's eastern coast and inland. The Kanem-Bornu people in the region of Lake Chad (bordered by what are today Nigeria, Niger, Chad, and Cameroon) adopted Islam in 1086.

Over the next few centuries, European merchants intensified their development of African coastal trading posts. They were eager to send back ivory (elephant tusks), gum, timber, cocoa, animal hides, and other native products that commanded high prices at home.

They were forever seeking gold and diamonds, and Africa yielded a quantity of those and other precious stones. If these items were hard to come by and to extract, the traders knew of another commodity that could always be had with relatively little effort and expense. It was the "product" that has made cruel merchants wealthy throughout human history: slaves.

Some of the newcomers had nobler ideals in mind. They thirsted for knowledge of the earth's unknown regions. Some felt it their moral duty to introduce others to Christianity and to the benefits of Europe's scientific and medical discoveries.

Today, however, most historians and social commentators concur that the European influence in Africa brought more harm than good. For one thing, colonial development created rapid economic growth that eventually collapsed after the colonies became independent. Today, for example, the country of Nigeria finds itself at the mercy of unpredictable world oil demands and other outside pressures that profoundly affect daily life among Nigerians.

People of Fanti, c. 1883 *The Fanti lived along the Gulf of Guinea. The head, or chief, of each Fanti state was chosen from a royal lineage. The several states never united. Each remained autonomous, forming alliances in time of war. Traditional Fanti religion included belief in a supreme creator and in lesser deities who derived their power from him. The worship of ancestral spirits was also important. In the late 20th century, most Fanti were converted to Christianity.*

THE SLAVE COAST

From the 15th to 18th centuries, Europeans knew the lower coast of West Africa not by country names, but by trade names. These stemmed from the commodities that made each area famous.

Africa in 1876 *Africa is the second largest continent, after Asia, covering about one-fifth of the total land surface of the Earth. The continent is bounded on the west by the Atlantic Ocean, on the north by the Mediterranean Sea, on the east by the Red Sea and the Indian Ocean, and on the south by the combined waters of the Atlantic and Indian Oceans. Highlighted on this map is the Gulf of Guinea area, the western edge of Africa. The tectonic plate here, that is the structure of the Earth's crust, is remarkably similar to the area of South America running from Brazil northward to Guyana and Surinam. The almost exact geology of these two coastlines is one of the closest confirmations of the theory of continental drift, the large-scale movements of continents during one or more epochs of geologic time.*

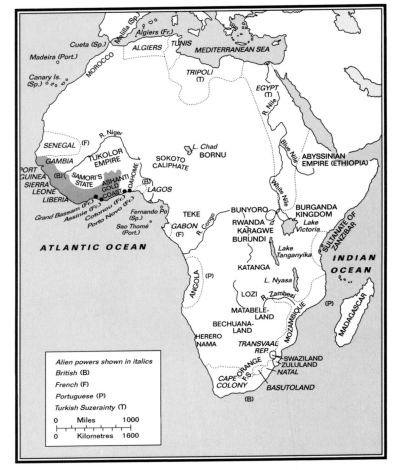

First, in the vicinity of Cape Palmas, was the Grain Coast. This was what is now the country of Liberia, founded in the 19th century by freed slaves. Agriculture remains its major economy.

Just inside the Gulf of Guinea, as a ship began skirting eastward from the open Atlantic, was the Ivory Coast. Côte d'Ivoire (French for Ivory Coast) is the name of that African nation today. Its best-known export, obviously, was elephant tusks.

Next, at what is now the nation of Ghana, came the Gold Coast. Gold is still one of Ghana's chief mineral resources, along with diamonds and various ores.

The Emir of Gombe, 1904 *Gombe, on the Gongola River in northeastern Nigeria, was mainly inhabited by the Fulani people. The area prospered until the 1880s, when religious warfare and the encroachment of the British brought severe economic and political disruption. Today, Gombe is a major collecting point for peanuts and cotton, especially since the opening of the railroad in 1963. Population (2000 est.) 100,000.*

Zamfara Men, 1912 *The Zamfaran people are related to the Hausa. Their territory lay above the confluence of the Niger River and the Benue River (in present-day northern Nigeria). Isolated until the 14th century, the Zamfaran were then converted to Islam by missionaries from Mali. The British gained trading privileges in this area through an 1885 treaty, but the Zamfaran strenuously opposed further colonial expansion. In 1903, however, British military forces incorporated the Zamfaran people into the protectorate of Northern Nigeria.*

Finally, along the beaches of today's Togo, Benin, and southwestern Nigeria, came the colonial territory whose name inspired chilled silence then as now: the Slave Coast. For two centuries, until the early 1800s, it was from here that most of the slaves captured and sold to Europeans in West Africa exited their home continent in chains.

The need for laborers on western plantations arose shortly after the Spaniards invaded the West Indies and the Americas. Portuguese slavers began supplying Spanish grandees there with African slaves in the early 1500s. English, French, and Dutch colonists also established plantations. Import crops much in demand in Europe included sugar and rice, and the planters found the rich subtropical soil of the Indies, southern North America, and South America excellent for growing them. Their great problem was that sugar cane and rice production was extremely labor intensive.

Accordingly, the slave trade from West Africa multiplied. African kings and native merchants rounded up farmers and fishers and sold them at the Europeans' coastal trading posts. It has been estimated that 275,000 black slaves were shipped in chains to different countries during the 1500s, 1,340,000 during the 1600s, and more than 6,000,000 during the 1700s.

In addition, African traders transported slaves from the sub-Sahara regions northward across the great desert to Mediterranean ports. Slave holding was also common within Africa itself. According to estimates, in the 1800s the Muslims' Sokoto Caliphate, in what is today northern Nigeria, had more slaves than any foreign country except the United States. Elsewhere in the Niger region, the Yoruba and neighboring ethnic groups engaged slave labor to transport palm oil and other products to the European trading posts. Slaves were forced to row river canoes and dugouts and to carry merchandise, loaded on their heads, overland.

Altogether, an estimated 3.5 million slaves were taken from the territory that today is Nigeria. They include people from the Ibo, Yoruba, Hausa, Ibibio, and other cultures.

Ending the Atlantic Slave Trade

The conscience of the European powers eventually prevailed. Denmark became the first European country to abolish its slave

trade in 1792. England banned slavery in 1807, after a long, bit-
ter abolition campaign led by evangelical Christians in that
country. The British government, in turn, began to exert pressure on its overseas colonies and on other nations to do the
same. England even posted a permanent naval blockade off the
West African coast to catch slave ships and rescue their human
cargo. It has been estimated that during the 1830s, a sixth of the
Royal Navy's ships were patrolling West African waters on the
lookout for slavers. If tried and convicted by a British court,
slave traders faced the death penalty.

France became slave free in 1848; the Netherlands, in 1863.

It took longer to abolish slavery in the countries that received
and worked the prisoners. Although the United States began
passing laws to curtail the importing of slaves in the early
1800s, Americans living in both the South and North continued to own them. It was not until the American Civil War
(1861–1865) that slavery effectively ended in the United States.
Slavery continued to be accepted in Brazil until 1888.

Despite the growing tide of abolition during the first half of
the 1800s, almost 2 million additional slaves were taken from
Africa during that century. Today, slavery is officially banned
by most nations, but it is not unknown.

A question that baffles history students today is why African
kings and merchants would sell their own people into bondage.

Money is said to be the root of all evil. In this instance
that clearly was true. The local strongmen were enticed by
certain of the goods the Europeans had to offer, especially
firearms, cloth, liquor, and various types of metals unknown
to the natives.

The kingdom of Oyo was a leading exporter of slaves.
Another was the state of Aro, whose merchants held trade fairs
and markets across the interior of the Niger region. Human
commerce accounted for much of the traders' income.

An example of a smaller African kingdom that turned to
slave trading for prosperity was the Ijaw state along the coast.
For many generations, the Ijaw had been predominantly fishers,

The King of Gobir and His Attendants, 1898 *The Hausa people developed a number of centralized states in the northern plains of Nigeria—Daura, Katsina, Kano, Zaria, Kebbi, and Gobir—each with a walled city, a market center, and a monarchical system of government. Islam was introduced from the Mali empire during the 14th century. There was considerable rivalry among the Hausa states over agricultural lands and the control of trade and trade routes. Between 1897 and 1903, British military units conquered this area.*

living in small seaside villages. They netted fish off the coast, dried them, and traded them—along with salt—to peoples in the interior. With the coming of the European slave ships, Ijaw leaders formed pacts with Aro traders, becoming intermediaries and offering market facilities to the slaving parties.

THE MISSIONARIES

As noted, growing Christian protests during the 1700s, mainly in Great Britain, hastened the downfall of slavery. The same Christian zeal that gradually arose, primarily among England's Protestant denominations, was to have a further impact on relations between Europeans and Africans. Ardent Christians believed all humans should not only be free from bondage but be exposed to the message of the Scriptures.

Efforts to spread the Gospel were not new. Churches that were established in American settlements and colonies of the 15th and 16th centuries were initially intended to serve the spiritual needs of the European intruders themselves. In addition, however, one of Spanish Queen Isabella's driving motives in dispatching Columbus and other explorers across the Atlantic was to convert the natives they encountered. (In practice, the Spanish conquistadors and colonists from other nations spent most of their time searching for gold or struggling to survive. They didn't permit the work of the priests to get in the way of prosperity.)

Catholic clergy, primarily from Spain and Portugal, were at work continuously in the Americas, in Asia, and in coastal Africa throughout the 16th and 17th centuries. In the late 1700s and early 1800s, they were joined by new Protestant missionary societies. The first such organization to reach the Niger area was the Church Missionary Society (CMS) of the Church of England.

This expanding global movement by the Protestants, in turn, inspired Catholic leaders in France, Spain, and elsewhere to expand their own missionary efforts. Increasing exploration and trade around the African continent naturally began to focus the different denominations' attention in that direction. The missionaries were not competing against each other. This land was vast. In the Niger area each organization found an unvisited section of the river basin to settle. CMS emissaries found themselves working among the Yoruba people; Catholic priests, among the Ibo.

Once the Protestant societies were organized, it took many years for them to take a foothold on foreign coasts and much longer to infiltrate the interior of Africa. When they did, toward the end of the 19th century, they became extremely influential in the developing relationship between the Africans and the European visitors.

The missionaries were willing to go to places and endure hardships that the profiteers had avoided. Compared to the often harsh ways of the traders, the Africans found the missionaries to be friendly guests. More quickly than colonial governments, the mission societies recognized the importance of working with rather than over the natives. They placed locals in charge of much of the work and of decision making—a practice that became known as the "native church" policy.

By the 1820s the CMS had appointed the first black Anglican bishop of the Niger region: Samuel A. Crowther. Crowther, a member of the Yoruba people, had once been a slave. After being educated and ordained in Britain, he returned to his homeland with the earliest Anglican missionaries.

The European governments recognized the value of the missionaries to their colonial efforts. For the most part the clergy were accepted by the natives and could speak the African languages. They established schools and hospitals for the natives, and they were respected. They thus were excellent intermediaries between European and African leaders.

Many natives sensed that certain missionary establishments were, in a way, acting as agents of the outside rulers; but they accepted the missionaries' message. These natives organized their own Christian churches, independent of the CMS and other European societies.

EXPLORING THE INTERIOR

One historian observed that to the typical European of 1800, "Africa was little more than a coastline." Even in the late 1800s, most European trade was limited to the fringes of the continent. The white colonists—some of them former slaver dealers—operated trading posts along the coast and on the banks of major rivers. Meanwhile, much of the trading was actually done aboard ships at anchor offshore.

The Europeans depended on native middlemen to bring them goods from the interior. For the whites to mount expeditions and search for African commodities themselves wasn't cost-effective. Besides, the white traders were not eager to expose themselves to the continent's strange diseases and often difficult terrain. They were not accustomed to the hot, humid climate. The mosquitoes that swarmed over the waterways were unbearable. Unknown fevers stymied European doctors; one Niger River expedition in the 1840s lost a third of its personnel to disease.

The Europeans also worried about possible attacks from hostile natives if they ventured inward. The African middlemen, to be sure, discouraged white expeditions from going inland. The middlemen could obtain trade goods easily and cheaply in the interior and sell them at a much higher price on the coast. They aggressively protected their role in this lucrative arrangement.

BRITAIN TAKES CHARGE

Britain in the mid-1800s staked its claim in what is today Nigeria. A government consulate was set up in 1848 to oversee British interests in the Gulf of Guinea, particularly the Niger delta. In 1861 Britain established a colony at the port of Lagos.

The threatening inroads made by rival European explorers like Heinrich Barth pressured the English to set up an official presence there. Barth, a German, brought back detailed notes from his adventures into the Sokoto Caliphate in the northern

Emir Abbas of Kano and His Royal Court, 1912 *In 1903 the British appointed Abbas the emir of Kano. During his reign (1903–1919), the British insisted that village heads be paid a fixed salary rather than the customary percentage of the taxes they collected. This changed the entire native administrative system into a modern bureaucracy. There were more than 4,500 such units of various sizes within the Kano jurisdiction.*

Niger area. Was it possible the Prussians had designs on this rich river basin? The British would take no chances.

Englishman George Goldie, called the Founder of Nigeria, lived from 1846 to 1925 and was knighted in 1887. The West African area he brought under England's control (which he originally referred to as "the region of Niger") was seven times the size of England itself. Some of his admirers thought it should be named Goldesia, but Goldie—a man who scorned publicity—rejected the notion. (The name that ultimately was chosen, Nigeria, is of course a tribute to the great river. It was suggested by English journalist Flora Shaw.)

In 1877 Goldie first set out with his brother to explore the Nigerian interior. That trip had to be aborted when his brother contracted a dangerous fever on the Niger River.

In 1878 many British trading companies operated along the coast, particularly around Lagos and the Niger delta area. The most prominent ones were Alexander Miller Brothers, the West African Company, the Central African Trading Company, and James Pinnock and Co. Their agents typically were rough and ruthless operatives who stopped short of little in "persuading" native merchants to agree to their contracts.

A chief export back home was palm oil and related palm products, valuable for food preparation, soap making, and as a lubricant for machinery. (At that time, petroleum-based products were not commonly used in mechanical operations, as they are today. Thus, such lubricants as palm oil and sperm oil from whales were major items of commerce.) The English companies shipped some £300,000 worth of palm products to Europe each year. Palm oil was such an important item of trade that the Niger delta became known as the Oil Rivers.

Palm products were valuable to the Niger basin natives as well as to the Europeans—but not necessarily for the same reasons. Among other things, the Africans used palm kernels as a food source, they made palm wine, and they used the palm fronds as a building material for constructing huts.

GOLDIE LEAVES HIS MARK

For years native Africans had acted as middlemen for European traders, bringing goods from the interior to the coast. The invention of the steam engine, probably more than anything else, changed that. European merchants began using the new steam-powered watercraft to probe the Niger River themselves in their quest for ivory, palm oil, and other goods. They no longer had to pay the middlemen. This angered some of the interior tribes, who began raiding the trading expeditions.

The British companies faced another growing threat. French traders were claiming rights to some of the same territory.

Goldie convinced the British trading companies to merge. There would be strength in union, he knew. The result was the National African Company. In 1886 Great Britain designated Nigeria a separate colony and chartered Goldie's commercial enterprise as the Royal Niger Company.

Interestingly, the charter required the company to abide by native customs "except so far as may be necessary in the interests of humanity." Apparently, this clause was intended to guarantee that slave trading by local chiefs would be opposed by British officials, as would other traditional customs the visitors considered inhuman.

Goldie proved to be a shrewd, ambitious trade leader. Over a 10-year period he and his colleagues negotiated some 200 treaties with African tribes. Basically, they acquired official ownership and control of each tribe's domain. In return, the British promised only to pay a "a reasonable amount" and to protect the tribe from unfriendly neighbors. Twenty British gunboats along the Niger River enforced the treaties, sometimes shelling the villages of natives who attacked trading posts.

Perhaps Goldie's character is revealed by the fact that he did not establish the Royal Niger Company's base of operations conveniently on the coast, but rather at Lokoja. Lokoja is located a third of the way into the heart of Nigeria, where the Benue River merges with the Niger River. Although situated an uneasy distance from British naval support posted in the Gulf of Guinea, Lokoja was a strategic trading location.

Some historians regard Goldie as an opportunist who, like other Europeans in Africa, took advantage of the natives and often treated them cruelly. No one questions his courage. Goldie sometimes would meet with tribal chiefs around their own fires, surrounded by potentially hostile warriors.

Goldie once described a banquet to which he was invited by a powerful chief. The chief suffered from leprosy. Leprosy, a disease that mutilates the skin and damages the nerves, is contagious. Until modern treatment became available, victims of it in many cultures were forced to exist in dreaded, isolated leper colonies. When the chief, in a gesture of unity, took a piece of meat from his platter and held it out between his deformed fingers for Goldie to eat, the Englishman naturally paused—but only for a moment. Goldie's desire for a treaty outweighed his personal health concern. He ate the food, affirming the bond between him and his host.

In 1894 the British expanded their official holdings, announcing the formation of the Niger Coast Protectorate. This broad territory extended as far up the Niger River as Lokoja. (Different from a colony, a protectorate was overseen directly by the British Foreign Office.) Obviously, Great Britain was increasing and strengthening its claim to the Niger basin.

Three years later Goldie accompanied a British-led force of native soldiers into the interior. Their goals were to oppose the growing French trade to the west and to thwart African slavers—natives who captured individuals from rival tribes and sold them into bondage. The British-led native troops were well disciplined and effective. They conquered two Muslim slave-trading states, Nupe and Ilorin. Goldie's trading company was unable to control those territories because of their size, so the British government took them over.

In 1899 the British terminated the Royal Niger Company's charter and Goldie returned to London. During his years with the Royal Niger Company, he had effectively kept the Germans

Hausa Soldiers, c. 1883 *These Hausa soldiers are wearing British military-type caps and using British cannons. They were probably recruited by George Goldie's Royal Niger Company to combat French commercial competition along the Niger River.*

and French out of the important river delta. To his credit, Goldie had supported the principle of native Africans ruling their own continent. (He presumed, of course, that the native leaders would be acting under the general control of the British.) Despite that, however, Goldie is probably most widely remembered as the Englishman who "forced open the Niger" for European trade.

The Palace of the Emir of Kano, c. 1900 *Several thousand people lived in the emir's palace; all were loyal to him through vows of unconditional obedience. Traditionally, such allegiances became institutionalized through hereditary slavery, although this term does not accurately describe this complex symbiotic relationship. The emir chose his servants, court attendants, city gatekeepers, and confidants from these palace people.*

A FRAGILE RULE

Until 1914 British holdings in the Niger basin were administered as two separate protectorates: north and south. Each had its own colonial governing staff. Even after a unified Nigerian administration was established that year, lower levels of government were maintained in the separate regions for day-to-day decision making and the keeping of order.

In fact, after 1914, the practical running of the colony was conducted in not two but three distinct geographic regions: north, east, and west. This general system of regional government continued even after Nigeria gained its independence half a century later.

To take charge of its territory in Nigeria, England in 1899 dispatched a veteran army commander, Frederick Lugard, as high commissioner. Lugard (1858–1945), a gaunt-faced soldier with a long, wavy mustache, had already earned respect in other parts of Africa as well as in the Niger region. He had helped Goldie secure the Niger region from the French several years earlier. (Lugard, incidentally, married journalist Flora Shaw who, as noted earlier, gave Nigeria its name.)

Lugard had only about £100,000 in his treasury for establishing and controlling the sprawling Niger region. Most of this land was unknown to Europeans. It contained an estimated 10 million people. Under Lugard were five administrative officials and about 100 staff personnel. He was given a force of several thousand native soldiers, commanded by British officers.

The British, plainly, were weak on resources. Had they wanted to, any of several native kingdoms in and around Nigeria could have opposed Lugard with armies numbering into the tens of thousands. The British were confident in their modern weapons and well-trained soldiers, but they had to be cautious. In the words of one historical account: "One serious defeat, or even a successful ambush, could have wiped out the entire armed force of most early colonial governments."

At first, controlling an African colony simply meant the British governors needed to control the British who lived there. If they could maintain order in their coastal and river posts, they knew, they basically could leave the natives alone and could begin to influence—and ultimately dominate—the locals through peaceful negotiations. Once the British began to control trade, they could impose taxes on the natives. Then, the British hoped, the colonies could become self-supporting without regular funding by the government in London.

LUGARD USES FORCE

Lugard understood this strategy. As a military commander, however, he believed force was necessary to subdue the native kingdoms in his protectorate. In particular, he eyed the powerful Fulani and Muslim states in the Sokoto Caliphate of the northern plains. They had established strong trading systems, partly built on slave raiding among neighboring peoples.

In 1902 Lugard captured the northern cities of Kano and Sokoto in surprise attacks, using machine guns and artillery against natives armed mostly with spears and swords. Within the next few years, he defeated all but one of the states and tribes.

He didn't try to rule them—at least, not directly. He simply replaced their once-independent emirs and chiefs with native leaders of his own choosing who were agreeable to the British plan of development. The Islamic court called the *sharia* continued to function in the north, resolving personal disputes among the Muslims. To ensure peaceful relations with Muslim subjects, the British curtailed the work of Christian missionaries in that part of the territory. Hausa was designated the official language of the northern region. Lugard and his officials did not want to challenge the age-old Muslim way of life.

As long as the emirs cooperated with the powerful British occupiers, they were allowed to keep their titles. In fact, some of them became paid officials of the colonial government. On the surface, native leaders appeared to be in control. But they looked for approval to the British, understanding all too well the power of modern European weapons.

British control didn't come without cost. In the village of Satiru, natives armed with axes and hoes massacred a force of 70 black soldiers and a British officer, as well as two civilians. Lugard responded by sending a column of 500 infantrymen, supported by the friendly sultan of nearby Sokoto, against

Emir Abbas of Kano, 1908 *Following the* Kano Chronicle *(written down in the 1890s), the best-known native history of the Hausa people, the Kano kingdom was founded in 999 by the grandson of the legendary father of the Hausa. According to tradition, each emir is his descendant. Missionaries from the Mali empire introduced Islam to the Kano region in the 1340s.*

A Gate of the Kano Wall *The wall of the city of Kano had fourteen gates. In 1903 British troops entered through the gate shown here and conquered Kano. This Hausa city, famous for its arts and industries, commerce, wealth, and strategic position in the trans-Saharan trade, came under British colonial rule.*

Satiru. They slaughtered an estimated 2,000 men, women, and children. This act of vengeance alarmed government officials in England, who feared the reaction of rival European powers.

Lugard had plenty of critics at home. Among them was a young statesman named Winston Churchill, who, during World War II, would become England's most famous prime minister.

Churchill complained that Lugard had set himself up as a self-styled "czar" of Nigeria.

Worldwide colonization had been opposed by some members of Parliament for many years. In 1865—just four years after Lagos was designated a British colony—one government report advised that the English pull out of West Africa. The critics argued that colonies like those in Africa were too expensive for England to control effectively.

The task was complicated. Although the British were able to oversee cooperative Muslim emirs in the north, this kind of arrangement did not work in all areas of the river basin. In some situations, unable to forge a relationship with native administrators, the whites took it upon themselves to perform the daily duties of government. This antagonized some of the local people—planting the first seeds of opposition to British control in the colony.

Under pressure from the home government, Lugard resigned his post in Nigeria in 1906 and accepted a less prestigious appointment as governor of Hong Kong. Later, however, he returned to Nigeria, helping bond the southern and northern protectorates into a unified colony and serving as its governor from 1912 to 1919. After World War I, he worked with the League of Nations for many years.

Hugh Clifford, who became governor of Nigeria in 1919, favored even greater representation by the natives in their own government affairs. He also encouraged Europeanstyle business development, especially among the people in the southern part of the colony. His stated objective for Nigerians was "general emancipation." Clifford was wary of the northern emirs, believing them to be too entrenched in "backward cultural conditions" to cooperate in his plan for the colony.

Under British Command

By the time World War I ended in 1918, the Europeans effectively controlled their African colonies, for the most part. Troubling tribal resistance had been put down. The colonists

Baro, c. 1908 *Baro was originally a small village of the Nupe people in west central Nigeria, about 400 miles from the sea. In 1906 the British chose it as Nigeria's link between rail and river transportation. The 350-mile Baro–Kano railway was completed in 1911. It was shortly eclipsed in importance by the railroad from Kano through Minna to Lagos that crossed the Niger at Jebba, 150 miles from the sea. From July to March, Baro is still used to ship peanuts and cotton by boat and barge to the Niger delta ports.*

(using native labor) had opened many miles of roads and railroads and had improved water transport in the continent's interior, connecting not only the cities within each colony but also making it much easier to travel and trade between territories.

For Nigerians, this made it easier to export palm oil, ground nuts, timber, and other products from the interior to the coast. In terms of economic development, Nigeria was prospering.

It was a curious way to run a colony. To an extent, the British could assign "two or three British officials at an outstation to rule 100,000 natives," as one 1935 government report put it. How much "ruling" they actually did depended on one's viewpoint. There was no way the whites could even begin to travel around their appointed territories to oversee daily details. If a military or law enforcement problem arose that was too serious for a local garrison to control, reinforcements could be brought in quickly. Native soldiers, not Englishmen, however, did the enforcing. The colonial armies were commanded by European officers but relied almost totally on native infantrymen.

The Europeans had weapons far superior to those of the Africans. Beginning in the early 20th century they also had air power. In the event of a serious revolt, the Europeans could respond by annihilating thousands of insurgents, if they so chose. But that, they knew, was not the way to keep a peaceful, productive colony, in the long run. Cooperating with native leaders and making them part (although an unequal part) of the colonial establishment was far better. If the natives seemed uninterested in cooperating, a dramatic display of "magic" in the form of modern weaponry often sufficed.

In this manner the British were able to exert a degree of control over Nigeria and even to extract taxes from the natives. Living under the thumb of foreign rulers was not new to most Africans. Throughout history they had been forced to pay homage to powerful invaders from the Middle East and from other parts of their own continent. If these arrangements proved unbearable, they could choose to take to the bush or relocate to other territories.

A Comfortable Collaboration

When the outposts began growing in size and increasing in the Western comforts of the turn of the century, families of

British administrative and army leaders began to join them in Africa, as did other European civilians. The British nationals formed social clubs, segregated from the natives. A color bar was established between the colonial leaders and their African subjects.

The Europeans who went to Africa in the 1920s and 1930s could expect to find many (though certainly not all) of the comforts of home. Those comforts usually did not extend to the natives. Outside the mission settlements, for example, the governments provided doctors and medicine for their own officials and families, but not for all the people of the colony. As for educating the natives, the home governments were content to leave that in the hands of missionaries; they were little inclined to establish and pay for government schools.

The colonists left much of the actual daily governing to the Africans. Crimes and disputes were judged and settled in native courts. European magistrates could overturn native legal decisions on appeal, but there were not nearly enough magistrates to hear every case that arose. The Africans continued to perform marriages and funerals and to decide issues of property ownership, just as they had for many centuries before the Europeans came.

In the countryside and remote villages, many Africans hardly realized they were under European sovereignty. They were forbidden to make war on their neighbors, and they were taxed. Beyond that, life was little different from what it had been before. The tax was not great, and many who could not pay it were allowed to perform short terms of work for the government instead—helping construct roadways and rail lines, for example.

In short, most colonial governments exerted light control over their subjects. They lacked the military might to be continuously heavy-handed. As long as they could keep the peace and extract enough in taxes from the natives to support themselves without drawing the disapproval of the home government, the colonials were content. They believed they were doing the

What Brought Europeans to Nigeria?

Africans a favor. The League of Nations, which was formed after World War I, called on European powers to oversee remote regions until the natives could "stand on their own feet in the arduous conditions of the modern world." They considered themselves obligated to move the African people forward, in terms of health, agriculture, and education.

This colonial system seemed to work well—for awhile.

Nigerian Leopard Hunter, 1909 *The leopard is found throughout Africa south of the Sahara. It feeds upon any animal it can overpower but generally preys on small antelope and deer.*

2

Life in Nigeria During European Colonization

Remember the last time you visited a different town or a different school and how unsettling—but also exciting—it felt to be surrounded by complete strangers? Perhaps you've visited another country, where that feeling was *really* powerful.

Imagine being an explorer in centuries past. You step from your boat on the beach of a distant land. The uneasy stares of silent natives lined along the shore and peering from behind trees and shrubs are your first greeting. You realize no one else from your country or even your race has ever seen these people before. You are the first.

In the coming days and weeks, as you begin to get to know them, the natives paint a lasting picture in your mind. You will never be the same. You have glimpsed and experienced, in a small way, an entirely different way of life you never dreamed existed. In a sense it's like discovering the human race anew.

Richard Leakey, a noted conservationist and fossil finder in Kenya, has commented on that sensation. He describes "the thrill of being with people untouched and often unmoved by contact with Western or other technology based cultures. . . . With the contemporary revolution in technology, there will be few if any such opportunities again." For us today, there are no unrecorded cultures left on the planet. But the Europeans who first went to Africa found eye-opening peoples and fascinating customs at each bend in the river.

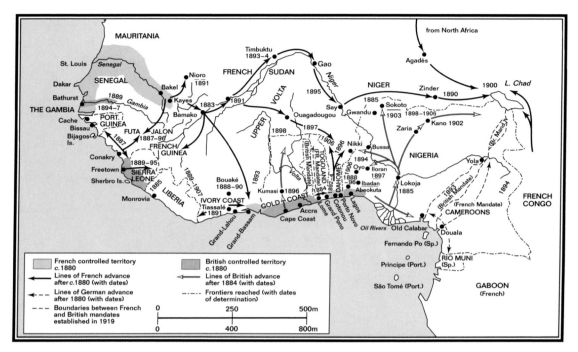

The European Advance into West Africa, c. 1880–1919
(after J. D. Fage, 1978)

A Changing Landscape

In the area of the Niger River, the newcomers saw a most interesting habitat. As it approaches the ocean, the river fans into a 14,000-square-mile delta—the largest river delta on the continent. Along the coast and on the delta islands are lush, thick mangrove rainforests, swamps, and lagoons. This terrain forms a coastal band extending from 10 to 60 miles inland.

The country's interior changes to seemingly endless woods and grasslands. The land becomes hilly and the elevation slowly increases to the Jos Plateau and, in the east toward Cameroon, the Adamawa Plateau. Vogel Peak, or Dimlang, Nigeria's highest elevation, is in the Adamawa Plateau. Although not unbearably hot, the climate is very humid. The summer temperature becomes up to 10 degrees Fahrenheit hotter as people travel northward and inland, away from the equator.

On the Jos Plateau begin some of the rivers that eventually feed the mighty Niger and, to the east, Lake Chad. Adding to the plateau's beauty are several waterfalls. These are not only

scenic; some provide hydroelectric power for towns and industries. Much of the industry here is mining. The plateau also supports agriculture. Butter and cheese come from its dairy farms; farmers carry their produce into the villages and cities to sell at open-air markets.

As we proceed north, the countryside opens into tropical grassland, dotted with trees, called a *savanna*. This vast, grassy plain is Nigeria's primary agricultural district.

North of the Niger River valley, in what today is the Republic of Niger, begins the great Sahara Desert, which blankets northern Africa. Modern Nigeria includes no desert land, but near its northern border with the Republic of Niger, it is semi-desert. Hot, dry winds, called *harmattan,* sweep down from the Sahara. The dry season in northern Nigeria lasts eight months.

As the landscape changes, so does the country's wildlife. The palm trees so valued by early European traders for their oil flourish along the coast, as do mahogany trees, ferns, and lovely flowers. Tamarind and baobab trees are common in the grasslands to

Dyeing Cotton Cloth in an Indigo Well, Offa, Southwestern Nigeria, 1898 *Offa is a Yoruba town in southwestern Nigeria. Cotton weaving and dyeing with locally grown indigo was and still is an important commercial activity in this area. The indigo plant is also extensively cultivated along the alluvial valley and plains formed by the Sokoto River in northwestern Nigeria.*

Washing in the Niger River, 1908 *The Niger River is the principal river of West Africa and of Nigeria. With a length of 2,600 miles, it is the third longest river in Africa after the Nile and the Congo. The river has been essential for the Nigerian economy. It is a tremendous resource for irrigation, shipping, and, since the 1960s, for hydroelectric plants.*

the north. Both varieties bear edible fruit; the bark of the baobab can be used for making rope, paper, and cloth.

Animal life along the coast is typical of swampy regions. Crocodiles, hippopotamuses and water snakes are common. Camels and predatory animals such as lions, hyenas, and leopards can be seen inland. We also find gorillas, chimpanzees, and giraffes. A wonderful variety of bird life flourishes in different regions. Most large, hoofed animals, however, are gone today.

Most of Nigeria's people live along the coast and lower rainforest area and in the northwest. Large areas of the country, especially in the northeast, have almost no human inhabitants.

THE RIVER

As is the case in many civilizations, rivers have influenced the lives of Nigeria's people throughout history probably more than any other factor. Nigeria has several rivers, including the Kaduna, the Sokoto and the Gongola. The principal one, however, is the one that gave the country its name.

For many centuries inhabitants have navigated the Niger River for trade and travel. Its native name is *gher-n-gheren*, which means "river among rivers." It is the third-longest river in Africa, after the Nile (the longest river in the world) and the Congo. Some 2,600 miles long and up to two miles wide in places, it is by no means contained within the country of Nigeria. It actually begins in Guinea and flows through Mali, Benin, and Niger. In southern Nigeria, approaching its delta on the Gulf of Guinea, it divides into channels that are so substantial they, in themselves, are called rivers and have their own names.

Passage on the Niger is thwarted in places by dangerous rapids. The country's seasonal changes in rainfall alter the depth of the river significantly, making river commerce more practical at certain times of the year than at other times. Today, as in the past, commercial and passenger transport provide lucrative livelihoods for Niger boatmen.

The Niger was virtually unknown to Europeans until the explorations of Mungo Park in 1795 to 1797 and 1805 to 1806. Outsiders believed the Niger flowed from east to west; Park

The Market at Lokoja, 1908
The river port of Lokoja is situated on the west bank of the Niger River, opposite the mouth of the Benue River. British merchants established a trading post at the confluence of these rivers in the 1850s. In 1860 the Scottish explorer William Balfour Baikie founded Lokoja. Balfour's travels to Nigeria helped to open the country to British trade. Besides being an important commercial town, Lokoja became the site for the first British consulate in the Nigerian interior (1860–1869). It was also the military headquarters for George Goldie's Royal Niger Company.

The Bussa Rapids, Niger River, 1898 *The Bussa Rapids extend for about 50 miles near Jebba in western Nigeria. Before the construction of the Kainji Dam and Reservoir (1969), the rapids were a major obstacle to navigation along the Niger. Today, the Kainji is the largest of several dams on the Niger. Each provides electricity to its surrounding area.*

proved the opposite to be the case. Park's first expedition was supported by the African Association, which later became Britain's world-renowned Royal Geographical Society. Its interest heightened, the British government underwrote Park's second trip up the Niger.

The river, with its perch, catfish, and carp, is obviously important to fishers. For centuries it has borne trade goods from the interior to the coast; rail and road commerce now connects with shipping at various points along the river. Niger waters are no less vital to livestock farmers.

In recent decades the Niger has been converted into a powerful source of hydroelectric energy and water for farm irrigation. Much of Nigeria's electricity comes from the dam at Kainji Lake.

EARLY CULTURES AND KINGDOMS

Our knowledge of ancient history in the region comes mainly from a few archaeological finds and from oral literature.

Nigerians today learn of their ancestors largely through the tradition of storytelling.

A fossilized skull and stone tools found in western Nigeria suggest human settlements in the area more than 10,000 years ago. On the Jos Plateau to the north, archaeologists found remnants of what is, to date, Nigeria's earliest known culture: the Nok people. They lived on the plateau from about 500 B.C. to A.D. 200 to 300. Africa's Iron Age possibly began here; relics include tools made of iron and burial items made of cast iron.

Other early cultures in the region include the Kanuri, who began the Kanem-Bornu empire in the ninth century A.D. near Lake Chad. The Kanuri were converted to the Muslim religion in the 11th century and expanded westward as far as the Niger. A notable characteristic of Kanuri towns was their U-shape, always open on the west end. Women wore their hair in a unique style, and they prepared their food unlike other area peoples, following traditions handed down from generation to generation.

Making a Roof, Northern Nigeria, 1908 *The traditional building materials used in Nigeria were mud, branches, cornstalks, leaves, and grass.*

Gateway in the Wall of Kano, c. 1900 *Kano is the Hausa capital city in northern Nigeria. In 1991 the Nigerian government placed the population of greater Kano city at about 600,000. The wall, which surrounds it, is more than 12 miles long, 40 feet wide at the base, and some 30 to 50 feet high. Inside the old city, along the Jakaka River, is the central Kurmi Market, a main caravan terminus. Modern Kano is a major commercial and industrial center. Peanuts, a local subsistence crop and now the prime export commodity, are bagged and stored in huge warehouses before being sent to Lagos for export.*

The Kanuri empire flourished, then gradually declined. It was infiltrated by and largely absorbed into other cultures, such as that of the Hausa-Fulani, by the mid-1800s. In modern times many Kanuri descendants speak the Hausa language and have changed to Hausa customs of dress.

Long before the first Europeans came, the Niger region was divided into ethnic kingdoms, or states. The Yoruba, Ibo (Igbo), Hausa, Fulani, and other powerful kingdoms, as well as many smaller states, evolved in different territories.

The early Nigerians were village dwellers. Typically, the homes of the common people were clustered around those of the elders and kings. The village was surrounded by fields of crops. Some people, such as the Yoruba, lived in walled cities. European visitors to Africa told of wide city streets that were several miles long and sprawling royal courts.

The early inhabitants were also traders. By A.D. 1000, historians believe, North Africans along the Mediterranean Sea, from present-day Morocco in the west to Egypt in the east, were exchanging goods via caravans across the Sahara Desert. Their trading partners were tribes who lived across the middle of the continent, including those of the Niger basin. Commodities included ivory, weapons, jewelry, salt, cloth, and slaves.

While we think of native African armies historically as bands of spear-throwing warriors, it's worth noting that in certain areas of the Niger basin, cavalry forces played vital roles in combat. A significant example was the Yoruba kingdom of Oyo, which was situated in an open savanna area where cavalry units could prove decisive.

What the Europeans Found

The Portuguese and other Europeans who went exploring found Africa peopled not primarily by hunter-gatherers, as was the case in the Americas and Australia, but by farmers. Archaeological evidence later showed that almost all of Africa had shifted from hunting-gathering to farming by the 10th century A.D.

These farmers were comparatively advanced, using iron tools. They were well organized into kingdoms and communities, protected by formidable armies of spear- and bow-wielding warriors. There was little the newcomers could teach them about trade; the Africans were already shrewd merchants with sophisticated trading networks that spanned the continent. They were truly international traders, moving certain of their goods over very long distances to faraway kingdoms.

Where possible, they used animals and boats to transport products. "Head loading," however, was the standard method of transport through the dense forests. Predictably, the traders focused on compact, light-weight luxury items, such as kola nuts and gold jewelry, rather than on staple goods. (Because the kingdoms were self-sufficient, they had little need to trade food and other necessities.)

Among the African kingdoms below the great Sahara Desert in the north, the area southwest of Lake Chad—which encompasses much of modern-day Nigeria—was apparently the leader in agriculture and in such handcrafts as metalworking and pottery making. Naturally, with coastal and river resources available, the people were also excellent fishers. For ages, control of the fishing and canoe trading along the Niger River was part of the power struggle among the Niger valley kingdoms.

The West Africans had sophisticated monetary systems. Money consisted of such items as cowrie shells (brought inland from the Indian Ocean), copper, iron, gold dust, certain types of cloth, and salt (obtained from the coast).

ONE NATION, MANY PEOPLE

If you travel from border to border in Nigeria and observe the marked changes in people, buildings, dress, religious practices, languages, and other features, you might be amazed that you have been in the same country the whole time. Few nations in the world have the cultural and social diversity found in Nigeria.

Nigeria's population comprises more than 250 native ethnic groups (estimates are as high as 400). Each is unique. Each speaks its own language and practices its own rituals and customs.

What do we mean when we talk of "ethnic diversity?" Scholars use several markers, or characteristics, to define ethnic divisions.

Language is the most obvious. People who speak a certain language usually consider themselves (and are considered by others) to be ethnically different from people who use other languages. Of course, in nations like Nigeria, many of the internal languages have substantial similarities. Should each one be identified as a separate ethnic division? What if speakers of two distinct languages in one part of the country consider themselves as belonging to the same ethnic group, but speakers of the same two languages in a different part of the country consider themselves as separate from each other? (This occurs in Nigeria among the Kanuri and Manga peoples.) These are questions for the linguistic and sociological experts—and not all of them agree in every situation.

Perhaps not surprisingly, in view of the recent century of colonization, English is Nigeria's official national language. It is, however, not spoken commonly outside the cities. Government officials and people educated beyond secondary school level typically speak both English and their ethnic language. In fact, many Nigerians can speak three or more languages.

For many centuries the ability to converse across linguistic bounds has been necessary for effective trade relations. Even before British mission schools became widespread around the turn of the century, many natives—especially along Nigeria's coast—learned a form of pidgin, or abridged, English, so they could carry on basic communication with white traders. Before the Europeans arrived, many people of the Niger basin were familiar with one or more languages spoken in neighboring kingdoms with which they traded.

Other ethnic markers include geographic location, religion, social organization, type of government, and the group's major form or forms of livelihood. Geography, next to linguistics, has been perhaps the most significant marker. Certainly in Nigeria, as one research group has reported, "the broadest groupings of linked ethnic units are regional." Even after the Niger area was united as a British colony, the English were wise enough to let the peoples of different areas continue to govern themselves according to ancient ethnic customs and rules. That system still applies today.

Of the hundreds of ethnic Nigerian cultures, 10 are predominant. Of those, the main ethnic groups are the Yoruba in the southwest, the Hausa-Fulani in the north, and the Ibo (or Igbo) in the southeast. Hundreds of smaller groups, speaking many different languages, live between and among them; and among

Yoruba Child, c. 1910

The Yoruba, one of the two largest ethnic groups of Nigeria, are concentrated in the southwestern part of the country, around the lower Niger River. Historically, the Yoruba shared a common language and culture but were probably never a single political unit. They eventually became the most urbanized Africans of the precolonial era, forming numerous hereditary kingdoms of various sizes, each of which was centered around a capital city. The traditional Yoruba religion had an elaborate hierarchy of deities, which included a supreme creator and some 400 lesser gods. Although some Yoruba are now Christians or Muslims, belief in their traditional religion continues. The Yoruba language has an extensive literature of poetry, short stories, and proverbs.

a given group, smaller cultural divisions often lead to disagreements. Let's examine each of these three primary groups.

THE CREATIVE YORUBA

White visitors soon recognized the Yoruba—the largest ethnic group on the western bank of the Niger River—as sophisticated

Hausa Fiddler and a Yoruba Headman c. 1900
More than 250 ethnic groups live in Nigeria. Each resides in an area that it considers to be its own by right of inheritance.

craftspeople. Their braided beads, wood carvings, and other works of art emphasized characteristics the Europeans knew and valued, such as bold eye appeal and symmetrical designs.

The Yoruba were skillful bronze casters, an art form they had obviously mastered centuries earlier. Archaeologists also found

A Yoruba Loom, c. 1883
The Yoruba traditionally have been among the most skilled craftspeople of Africa. They worked at such trades as leather crafting, glass-making, and weaving.

ancient stone and terra-cotta statues. Yoruba artisans worked with brass, as well.

Many of Nigeria's present-day leading artists, artisans, and authors are Yoruba. These people are also known internationally for their theatrical productions, which are written and performed in the Yoruba language but are received enthusiastically by audiences of all languages. Yoruba theater is based on modern political and social commentary, historical folktales and myths, religious themes, and ancient rituals. It incorporates traditional Nigerian music and costumes, giving viewers a glimpse of authentic Yoruba culture.

Making Pottery, c. 1898 *Most peoples of sub-Sahara Africa use pottery, many making it themselves. The preindustrial tradition involved the molding of fairly coarse-textured clay by hand. The pots so formed were then fired in open bonfires at a relatively low temperature. The variety of form and design is almost endless. Today, although the tradition of pottery making survives in many rural areas, city dwellers have switched to industrially manufactured wares.*

Before European colonization, the Yoruba had established a powerful kingdom, the Oyo Kingdom, sprawled between the lower Niger River and what is today the nation of Benin (Nigeria's neighbor to the west). Ifè, an ancient Yoruba city situated in what is now the state of Osun, was a center of trade, religion, and the arts.

An Oyo Court Messenger, c. 1910 *The Oyo live in southwestern Nigeria. They are related to the Yoruba people. An Anglican mission was established in Oyo in the 1860s. It is now St. Andrew's College (founded in 1897), the oldest teacher-training institute in Nigeria. The town was a traditional center of cotton spinning, weaving, and dyeing (with locally grown indigo). Oyo was also famous for carved calabashes (gourds). In 1888 British military forces occupied this area.*

The great Oyo kingdom fell apart into smaller, independent states during the 1820s. Ibadan, Owo, Abokuta, and other Yoruba cities struggled for control of the slave trade and of the commercial routes that passed through their territory. Ultimately, they all came under British control.

Today the Yoruba people are concentrated in the city of Ibadan in southwestern Nigeria, but the Yoruba language is spoken elsewhere. It is even used by some citizens of the nations of Benin and Togo. The Yoruba make up approximately 21 percent of Nigeria's population.

Ibadan, capital of the modern Nigerian state of Oyo, is an important "connector" city. Much of the trade between the port of Lagos to the south and the interior cities to the north passes by road and rail through Ibadan.

Ibadan, much more than a whistle-stop, is also the market center of local agriculture. Out of this area come palm oil, cacao, rubber, and timber products. Ibadan has a university, libraries, and other educational and cultural resources.

The Diverse Hausa

An estimated 10 to 15 million people make up the Hausa, who live mostly in northwestern Nigeria and southern Niger, Nigeria's neighboring country to the north. Hausa is the most widely spoken language in Nigeria. It is spoken not only among the Hausa people but in other states in the north. In fact, Hausa is spoken outside the Niger region; most cities of West African and Saharan countries have substantial Hausa language communities.

For centuries Hausa groups lived in city-states, under a form of feudalism. From about the 11th century A.D., the leaders of many of these cities were Muslim emirs; the city-states were called emirates. Each citadel had a royal ruling class, and the city-fortress was the area's center of trade, protection, and the settlement of disputes. Some city-states housed tens of thousands of citizens. People in outlying settlements came to the city to trade.

The emirates traded with one another. They also indulged in raiding and, at times, in open warfare. A complex system of alliances and enmities was established over the centuries.

During the 500 years before British colonization, these states were conquered by a succession of nearby kingdoms. The last conquerors were the Fulani people, today one of Nigeria's major ethnic groups. Under British rule a Fulani-Hausa political coalition was forged. It remains the primary ruling force in

Hausa Holy Man at Entrance to Sacred Water, 1914 *Although the Hausa accepted Islam in the 14th century, some pre-Islamic rites remained in their culture. Drinking water from a spring dedicated to an ancestral diety was such a ceremony.*

northern Nigeria. Despite past rivalries, there has been a significant blending of Hausa and Fulani cultures.

Today as many as half the people in this region live in small farming villages. Most of the Hausa people are subsistence farmers; they grow most of what they need to live on and trade

Hausa Man Playing a Stringed Instrument, 1898 *The Institutes of African Studies at the Nigerian universities of Ibadan and Ifè have done much to reawaken interest in traditional folk dancing and poetry. With the establishment of radio and television stations in all state capitals, programs featuring traditional music and dance, folk operas, and storytelling are available in some 25 languages. Because writing became common only after 1900 (except in the Muslim north) and because few educated Nigerians showed any interest in folk traditions until the 1960s, much of the country's culture is believed to have perished. Many ancient folk songs have been revived by popular singers, who use modern musical instruments to provide sounds that villagers can hardly identify with the songs they inherited from their ancestors.*

for the rest. For centuries they have traded with distant kingdoms, especially westward as far as the Atlantic coast and northward across the Sahara Desert. Many of their merchants have acquired great wealth.

THE TRAGIC IBO

In modern history the Ibo, or Igbo, people of southeastern Nigeria are known primarily for their tragic attempt to escape persecution from their Fulani-Hausa neighbors. In the late 1960s the Ibo made an unsuccessful attempt to form the independent nation of Biafra.

Like the Hausa, the early Ibo are thought by some historians to have been subsistence farmers, growing yams as their mainstay crop. Unlike other major Nigerian cultures, they are believed to have lived in small, independent villages, with no overriding political system. (Many of the old villages and cities are much larger today.)

Nevertheless, the Ibo were successful traders and skilled craftspeople. Scholars disagree about their cultural organization; some argue that Ibo culture at one time centered around the flourishing Nri kingdom. Some archaeologists believe the Ibo have lived in the "elbow" region of West Africa since prehistoric time. Rather than chiefs, the early Ibo chose priests to make important decisions for the group and settle disputes.

Today's Ibo people speak a Kwa language. Although concentrated in the southeast, sizeable Ibo minorities live in cities throughout Nigeria. These minorities typically live in their own ethnic neighborhoods.

Although British influences are woven into the local governments and even the lifestyles of Nigerians in many parts of the country, Iboland shows strong American characteristics. The Ibo value competition, business success, and personal achievement. The nation's first land-grant university, patterned after Michigan State University, was established at Nsukka. Class distinctions between the wealthy and poor is especially marked among the Ibo.

THE CHALLENGE OF DIVERSITY

Such an elaborate patchwork of ethnic diversity is at the same time wonderful and troubling. It gives Nigeria unusual strengths and potential while presenting uncommon problems.

Hausa Couple, Katsina, 1922

The pros and cons of ethnic diversity have always existed among the people of the Niger basin. Long before the Europeans arrived, the various tribes and kingdoms regarded one another with mistrust, scorn, envy, and fear. They sometimes fought and raided one another; they carried away human slaves.

Group of Hausa People, c. 1883 *The Hausa live in northwestern Nigeria and are mainly Muslims. Today, the Hausa language, which is infused with many Arabic words, is the official language of northern Nigeria and is used throughout much of western Africa as a second language.*

On the positive side, they also learned to get along; they traded. Those who farmed the earth and those who raised livestock knew the benefits of peaceful coexistence and communication. Crop farmers would buy cattle and pay the herders to raise the livestock to maturity.

Smaller groups were often known for one or two special products or talents. By exchanging these specialty goods and services, they found unity as a whole.

Even in warfare, aggressive kingdoms would forge alliances with certain villages within enemy territory. Genera-

Hausa Boy in Front of Traditional Hut, 1908

tions after the raiding episodes ended, the old alliances might be preserved.

CULTURAL RICHES

Nigeria draws a wide body of customs and art styles from its hundreds of ethnic groups. Today, these traditional native customs and art forms have meshed somewhat with outside influences—not just British but American as well and, from another direction, Arabic. Musicians like I. K. Dairo, for example, have popularized a form of music called *juju*. This fast-paced, casual sound combines both Western and African instrumentation with native religious and folk music. It has become very popular in Nigeria since independence and has even spread to America and Europe. If you listen closely, you will hear clear similarities between *juju* songs and those of the Caribbean.

Ibo Mask Used in Harvest Dances, 1925 *The Ibo people live mainly in southeastern Nigeria. Traditional Ibo religion included belief in a god of creation, an earth goddess, and numerous other deities and spirits. Before the European conquest, the Ibos were not united but lived in autonomous local communities. By the mid-20th century, however, a strong sense of ethnic identity had developed. In 1967 the Ibo-dominated eastern region of Nigeria tried to secede from Nigeria as the independent nation of Biafra. The civil war caused widespread death and destruction. Beginning in 1970, the Nigerian government sponsored reconstruction and relief programs to overcome the effects of the war. Many Ibo, including some who had fought with rebel forces, were given government positions.*

In the meantime, nurtured by university folklore programs, a great body of traditional poetry, art, crafts, theater, storytelling, and dance forms is being preserved. If we examine some of the tribal masks, ebony and thorn carvings, and paintings, we can glimpse the life and customs of the Niger region of old.

Nigerian art forms have found their way into religious services. African musical elements—and even dance—have been enfolded into religious expression.

An Ibo Relic, c. 1925
This relic was used for divination—that is, the practice of foretelling the future. This phenomenon is found in most cultures, both ancient and modern. In traditional Ibo religion, the will of the deities was sought both by divination and by the consulting of oracles. Today most Ibos are Christians.

NIGERIAN RELIGIONS

About half of Nigerians (primarily in the north) embrace the Muslim (Islam) religion. In 1804 Muslims began a *jihad*, or holy war, that lasted four years. The result was the union of northern Muslims and those in neighboring areas under one Islamic government, the Sokoto Caliphate.

The leader who instigated this *jihad* was Usuman dan Fodio. He was a Muslim scholar and *mallam*, or religious teacher, who

Kanuri Dancers, 1904

The Kanuri people lived in northeastern Nigeria. Their empire, called Borno, reached its zenith during the 16th century. The Kanuri have been Muslims since the 11th century. The political and religious leaders of the Kanuri traditionally surrounded themselves with much pageantry, including elaborate dances. Today, Maiduguri is the principal Kanuri city. Population (1991 est.) 282,000.

acquired a massive following as he traveled and preached among the Fulani people. He founded a capital city named Sokoto. At its height the Sokoto Caliphate was the largest empire on the African continent. After Usuman dan Fodio's death in 1817, the kingdom was divided.

Islam is evident today in northern Nigeria's daily life. Muslim prayers open and close public meetings. Traditional Islamic law is part of the regional judicial system. Cities and villages have mosques and other places for regular prayers. Those who can afford it still make the traditional pilgrimage, called the *hajj*, to the distant city of Mecca in Saudi Arabia. In modern times Muslim pilgrims from distant countries often make this journey by air, but some African Muslims still caravan across the northern African continent.

Muslim leaders typically come from long family lines of clerics, many of whom study in foreign countries. They become religious scholars, called *ulama*. The rich merchant class and ruling emirs throughout history have used *ulama* not only as spiritual mentors but as legal advisers. Some wealthy Muslims and members of certain other African religious sects still practice polygamy, in which one man has two or more wives.

Approximately a third of the people are Christians. Christianity is particularly common among the Yoruba and other people in the southern coastal areas, where the 19th-century missionary settlements were strongest. It was to the colony's southwestern coast that many freed slaves returned in the 19th century, bringing with them the Western influences they had acquired. It is not surprising, therefore, that Yorubaland would become Nigeria's most Westernized and Christian region.

At the same time many of Nigeria's Muslims and Christians still cling to ancient gods and rituals. Traditionally, Yoruba people worshiped many gods; these included, for instance, Shango, their god of thunder. Many Nigerians believe powerful forces—both good and evil—are exerted by certain animals, minerals, and plants. The native Aladura Christian church accepts rituals to ward off evil spirits sent against its people by practitioners of witchcraft.

Religious costumes are not uncommon in native churches. From early times, people of the region have used ceremonial masks, drum music, and dance forms to communicate with spirits. Spirits are believed to reside in the carved masks.

Since the time of early Niger civilizations, many natives believed the ghosts of their ancestors bound the family to a certain locale. As generations passed, the belief in these spirits affected trade and social activities, leadership roles, land holding, and even the location of home sites. Many natives consider themselves obligated to continue the ancient customs, which are believed to affect every aspect of life from diet to dress. They live under the watchful eye of the spirits of long-dead ancestors.

Natives also respected "spirits of place." Parents passed down to children the belief that certain rocks, trees, and even animals were sacred spirits. Often, if a tribe relocated to a different place, they would carry a sacred object with them to ensure continued health and prosperity. Of course, the new homeland would have spirit objects of its own; these were accepted along with the transported spirits.

Naturally, ethnic priests were always important to the natives. They offered prayers and sacrifices to the spirits and conducted age-old rites.

The British often decried the natives' religious and tribal rituals as barbaric. In 1897 an English consul received reports of appalling practices in Benin, a city some 60 miles from the coast. Natives there were allegedly making human sacrifices. En route to look into it, the consul and his staff were attacked and killed. Colonial forces responded by seizing the city and sending its native chief into exile.

Likewise alarming to the Europeans were the natives' trials by ordeal. Persons accused of certain crimes would be subjected to brutal, sometimes dangerous, tests of endurance and strength. These were prescribed by a certain spirit to the priest as a way of determining the individual's guilt or innocence.

The British scoffed at natives' healing methods, which were also in the hands of spiritual practitioners. The medicine men would sell roots, herbs, and charms as cures and protective devices. Some of the healers used sorcery in attempts to purge the evil spirits they said were causing the victim's affliction. Tribal diviners claimed to be able to look into the future and foresee good or tragic results of everything from long trading journeys to complex family matters.

Marital matches, property disputes, and other issues of daily life were often resolved by spiritual decrees said to be handed down through religious leaders. When either a calamity or a happy event occurred in a person's life, it was explained as an example of supernatural intervention.

From ancient to modern times, generations of Nigerian men have met in secret societies that claim spiritual connections.

An Entertainer, Katsina, 1898 *Following a centuries-old tradition, entertainers—dancers and musicians—performed in the main Katsina market. These people were available for hire by local merchants and their songs extolled the virtues of the merchants' goods.*

Hausan Rainmaker, 1925 *In Hausan society a rainmaker—that is, a person who attempts to produce rain—held his ritual position because of his age and genealogy. The rainmaker was also responsible for the well-being of his local village community.*

Their main objective has been to enforce traditional order, preaching against immorality within their communities.

Today, Nigerian religious groups continue to be divided geographically, much the same as in generations past. Muslims dominate in the north, Christians in the south, and a mixture in the central areas. Christian denominations include both Protestants and Catholics, as well as Africanized Christian churches. Protestant denominations are most widespread among the Yoruba; Catholicism, among the Ibo.

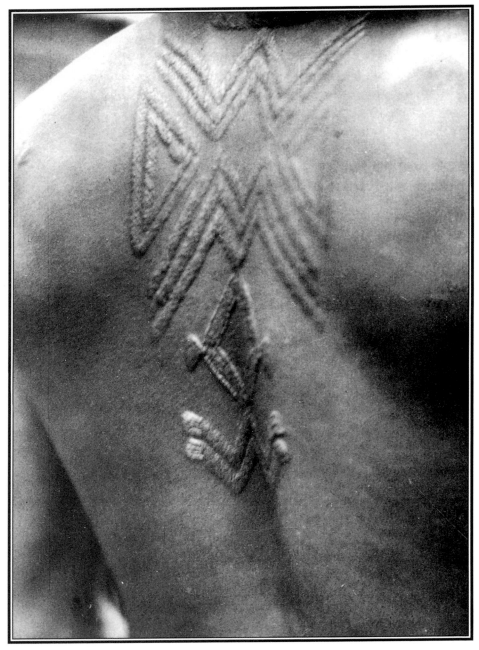

An Example of Cicatrization, 1925 *Cicatrization describes the scar formation at the site of a healing wound. This type of body decoration was frequently created for aesthetic reasons. Often, cicatrization was performed as part of marriage rites.*

3

RESULTS OF COLONIZATION

A SEPARATE CLASS

The British colonial leaders and nationals living in Nigeria and other British territories envisioned themselves as a separate class. This mind-set was different from that of the colonials in colonies controlled by other powers.

In the Belgian Congo, for example, the Belgian nationals wanted their African subjects to learn to become, in effect, Belgians. The French in Senegal saw the native Senegalese as prospective French citizens (for practical purposes, at any rate). But in the British colonies, most administrators never expected the natives to become Britons. It seemed best to let them remain Africans—as long as they agreed to abide by the will of England. As we saw earlier, in the colonies the British formed legislative councils with native representatives. This was wise diplomacy in a land in which the British ruling class formed a tiny minority.

Throughout the colonial period, relatively few European civilians settled in Africa. Most of those who did settle did so on the northern coast or in the southern part of the continent. Establishing a plantation or other business in Africa was an expensive undertaking for Europeans, filled with hardships and uncertainty. At the same time, there was little work to be had there for the European labor class because thousands of natives who would work for humble wages were available.

The original British colony at Lagos was an interesting blend of English Victorian attitudes, diverse customs and influences of native black leaders, and—oddly—new

An Egba Village, Near Abeokuta, Southwestern Nigeria, c. 1883 *Abeokuta was the capital of the Egba people. In 1851 the Egbas, aided by Christian missionaries and armed by the British, defeated a Dahomeyan army. The British then recognized the independence of the Egbas but broke this agreement in 1914 by incorporating the Abeokuta area into the protectorate of Nigeria.*

buildings in Brazilian-style architecture. Many of the residents there were freed slaves from Brazil and the Caribbean who had been brought back to their homeland. Some of them were given positions by the British colonial officials; some were appointed to the Lagos Legislative Council.

Barber Shaving Boy's Head in Front of Mud Hut, Northern Nigeria, 1898 *The walls of mud huts could be as much as three feet thick. Mud huts had two serious disadvantages: they were easily eroded by rain and mud is not resistant to termites.*

IMPROVING THE SCHOOLS

As we've seen, both before and during the colonial period, missionaries established the first schools in Africa. The colonial governments, operating with limited funds and staff, were content to let the missionaries see to educating African children.

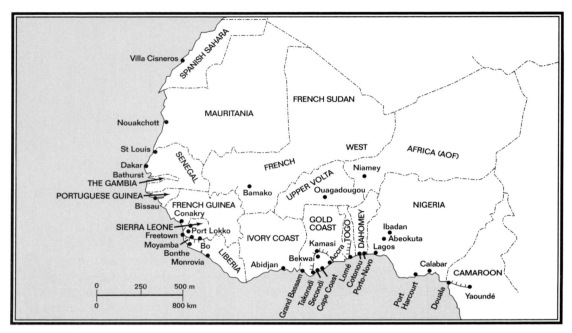

Politics and Nationalism in West Africa, 1919–35

In 1925 the British ordered their African colonial governments to begin helping and improving the mission schools and to conduct inspections. From then until World War II (1939–1945), it's estimated that about a fourth of the Africans in British colonies received at least two years of formal education.

The Europeans found the natives to be eager and intelligent students. They could learn to communicate and think like the Europeans and solve problems the way the Europeans did. It soon became apparent that, in time, the Africans would be perfectly capable of governing themselves in the European style—if they wanted to do so. The winds of independence were beginning to stir in the crude mission schools.

GROWING NATIONALISM IN THE NORTH, SOUTH, AND ABROAD

The mission schools flourished in the lower part of the Niger basin. Thus the native people gradually became Europeanized in the south. In the Muslim north, in contrast, the emirs reigned peacefully under British control, while maintaining their

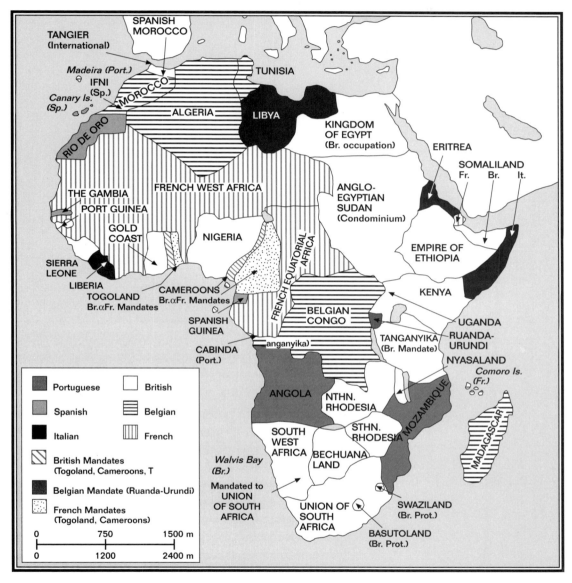

The Changed Map of Africa after the First World War *(after J. D. Fage, 1978)*

Another Example of Cicatrization *Among some Nigerian groups, cicatrization was used to indicate status or rank of an individual in a manner visible to the other members of society.*

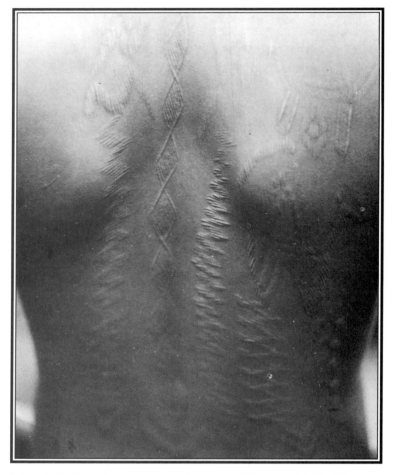

Islamic faith and customs as the central focus of daily life. Not surprisingly, anti-Western feeling was growing among the northern Nigerians.

At the same time educated citizens in the south were questioning British rule and, in their own way, were developing a growing sense of nationalism. The citizens of England, they reasoned, would never tolerate interference by foreign rulers. Why should it be different for the people of the Niger basin?

This feeling was developing not just against the British in Nigeria but against other European powers in other parts of the continent. A pan-African spirit—based on the logic that

Africans, not outsiders, should govern Africa—evolved between World War I and World War II. The movement was strengthened by African students studying at universities in England, America, and elsewhere. They formed student unions, arguing that colonial rule was shackling the great continent and keeping it from progressing with the rest of the world community. They also accused the European officials of ignoring the long-held cultural traditions of the local people.

Native Christian churches joined the opposition to colonial government. African Christians were unhappy that many missionaries refused to let them incorporate age-old tribal customs into their lives and worship. They were also frustrated by the Europeans' slow acceptance of native preachers. From independent native pulpits, criticism of colonial policies increasingly became part of the church teaching.

By 1930 Nigeria was nurturing a widespread and irrepressible sense of nationalism—although the people who felt this way were divided across the colony. They were to be found among ethnically diverse groups that had fought and shunned each other for many generations. Overcoming their internal differences would be a major hurdle in the 30-year movement toward independence.

STEPS TOWARD SELF~SUFFICIENCY

The British colonial system puttered along in Nigeria through the depression of the early 1930s and into World War II. The best the colonial administrators could expect was for their government to be self-sufficient. For the natives, customs and traditions and the overall way of life from generations past remained little changed.

After the war the British government established purchasing agencies and marketing boards for its West African colonies. These agencies guaranteed local farmers fixed prices for their crops. The locals began to realize a measure of economic security as part of the European commercial system, and the colonies overall grew stronger and more independent of support from their home countries.

Making Straw Plaited Rope, 1898 *Along the Nigerian coastland, houses were made of bamboo tied together with rope. Rope was made from the raffia palm, which abounds in this region.*

Meanwhile, the European conscience was aroused. It was obvious the natives needed better living conditions. They needed more hospitals and schools. They needed better homes with better sanitation. They needed more reliable communications. So Parliament allocated money for both economic and social development in Nigeria.

At the same time native Nigerians had been learning European ways of commerce and government—and learning to manage these affairs themselves. Here and in other colonies, they gradually developed a sense of native unity. Farmers

House in Arochuku, Southern Nigeria, c. 1925 *The Aro people bitterly opposed British authority in their area, where, for more than two centuries, they had held unchallenged political supremacy. The Aro had also earned enormous respect from neighboring tribes because of their guardianship of the famous Aro Chukwu religious oracle. At one point the Aro used their position to urge a total embargo on trade with all Europeans. In December 1901 British military units occupied Arochuku, hanged a number of chiefs, and destroyed the sacred oracle. The British conquest of the Aro was a major step in the extension of British authority over eastern Nigeria.*

formed associations in order to have a say in export policies and prices. Native lawyers, many of them educated in England, formed local associations, as did school teachers.

These organizations were not assaults on British authority. In time, however, they would help lead to an organized independence movement.

The cities, in the meantime, were swelling with people moving in from different small kingdoms, speaking different languages and dialects. They began meeting in common groups for support and recreation. As they encountered others who spoke different dialects of their language, these "clubs" broadened. In Lagos, a Descendants Union, for instance, was formed among various Ibo-descended citizens. Elsewhere, people with similar backgrounds organized musical bands, football clubs, and dance societies.

Workers were uniting to demand better conditions. Labor unions were not legally recognized, but as early as 1921, Nigerian workers were staging strikes. Many European labor contractors in Africa let their workers live in unsanitary, unsafe conditions and failed to pay their wages regularly. Some treated the natives cruelly. In Nigeria hundreds of workers reportedly died because of unhealthy conditions in the country's tin mines.

By the late 1930s Benjamin Nnamdi Azikiwe, who later became Nigeria's first president, was arguing for self-government in his newspaper, the *West African Pilot*. A few years later Azikiwe became secretary general of a new independence-minded political party, the National Council of Nigeria and the Cameroons (NCNC). Eventually, the NCNC drew members from more than 100 different ethnic groups, as well as from diverse professional, labor, and social organizations.

Another nationalist who used the power of the press was Herbert Macauley. His Nigerian National Democratic Party became popular in Lagos. Macauley expressed his views in his Lagos newspaper, the *Daily News*. He came to be regarded by some historians as the father of nationalism in Nigeria—perhaps because he ultimately became the NCNC party's first president. His influence, however, was never especially strong outside the port city; Azikiwe was considered the NCNC's leader. Therefore, in the middle of all the changes their European overlords had

An Elaborately Carved Wooden Door, Kano Area, 1898

brought them, the native Nigerians were discovering their identity as a related people, with roots thousands of years old.

TIDE OF INDEPENDENCE

Independence for the African nations began not far to the west of Nigeria. In 1957 the Gold Coast, a British colony, was granted independence and became known as Ghana. This was the result of a decade of tension, including African boycotts of European merchants and rioting in major cities.

In Nigeria, as we've seen, small political associations or debating societies had been organized decades earlier by the growing number of European-educated natives. They hoped eventually to bring the colonial government's executive and legislative councils under African control. Africans seemed to have little interest in *overthrowing* the colonial government; rather, their aim was to hold the majority of offices within the existing British system of government.

During World War II, soldiers from Nigeria and other British colonies served alongside British soldiers in different parts of the world. This experience opened the eyes of many native Africans. It demonstrated the concept of equality. If Africans could join the Europeans in war, why not in government? In fact, why couldn't they govern themselves?

The independence of Ghana heralded the demise of British colonial rule in Africa. Few doubted that Nigeria, Gambia, and Sierra Leone would soon become self-governing, as well.

The process took longer for Nigeria, primarily because it is much larger than Ghana. The Nigerian people lived in different regions of the country and had different standards of wealth and different views concerning social and political matters. Underneath it all were the timeless differences in their ethical values and beliefs. In many cases they distrusted one another.

During the 1940s the Yoruba in the southwest and the Ibo in the southeast jockeyed for control of the NCNC party. In 1951, after the Ibo rose to prominence within the party, some of the Yoruba contingent formed a new party called the Action Group. In Lagos growing political tension led to violent confrontations between the Yoruba and the Ibo.

While major ethnic groups like the Yoruba and the Ibo clashed with one another, they also faced divisions within themselves. The Yoruba, for example, were not a single, unified people with a common interest. Many of these internal divisions were (and remain) geographic in nature.

Even more divisive were the long-time differences between Nigeria's southern peoples and the mostly Muslim people in the north. The Muslim leaders formed their own political party, the Northern Peoples' Congress (NPC). Some British officials in the country encouraged hostility between the northern emirs and their southern neighbors. Many English leaders considered the northern Muslims to be friendlier than the southern political activists to the colonial government. There were even suggestions of making the northern territories an independent country. Other British leaders rejected the idea and worked for a unified Nigeria.

Step by step during the 1940s and 1950s, the British gave native Nigerians increasing control of local government bodies, planning commissions, and educational panels. In 1948 Britain officially published its intention "to guide the Colonial territories to responsible self-government within the [English] Commonwealth." It expected, of course, to preserve British interests in the colonies.

THE NATIONAL YOUTH MOVEMENT

The National Youth Movement (NYM) was organized in 1934 in the port of Lagos, and it soon had chapters in 20 towns. Its original purpose was to bring about better opportunities for higher education among the natives. As it grew, it broadened its goals and became a leading force in the nationalistic movement.

By the late 1930s NYM leaders like H. O. Davies were boldly proposing that Nigeria be made a member of the British commonwealth, with the same form of self-government as Canada. NYM members gained posts on legislative councils, and the organization became one of Nigeria's most prominent political groups.

In the early 1940s, as had occurred with other Nigerian political movements during the colonial era, the NYM split between different ethnic factions within the party, and the movement dissolved. Its aim to make Nigeria an independent commonwealth, however, did not die. Rather, that objective became a major plank in the NCNC's agenda after World War II.

During the 1950s more and more Nigerians came to realize that independence from British rule was close at hand. The political groups jockeyed for position to become the leading party in the soon-to-be-independent nation. They were faced with a double challenge: getting along internally within their own faction and getting along with the other groups.

INDEPENDENCE

In late spring 1957 the British government convened a conference in London to discuss how the hundreds of ethnic and political factions throughout Nigeria could be united into an independent state. It appointed commissioners to investigate the fears and concerns of the colony's various minority groups.

Between 1957 and 1959, territories in the east, west, and north of Nigeria were allowed to function under self-governing parliaments. They ultimately had to answer to the colonial government, based at that time in the capital at Lagos. Banking, communications, and colonial defense, for instance, still rested in the hands of the Lagos colonial officials. The regional parliaments, however, exerted most of the power within the three territories. They were even given control over how to use most of the tax revenue generated among their constituents.

On October 1, 1960, the English Parliament pronounced Nigeria an independent nation. Exactly three years later, it became the Federal Republic of Nigeria. It had its own parliamentary form of government, with the NCNC and the NPC as its major political parties. Azikiwe, the Ibo editor and nationalist who had become known to everyone as Zik, became the new country's first president. A leader from the Hausa culture, Abubakar Tafawa Balewa, was the new federal prime minister.

Nigeria's elected parliament consisted of a 44-member senate, selected by the new nation's regional government bodies, and a 312-member house of representatives, elected by popular vote. A national constitution provided the basis for regional government constitutions—although the regional documents called for different requirements and allowances. In the north, for instance, the local constitution contained provisions that upheld Islamic as well as national laws.

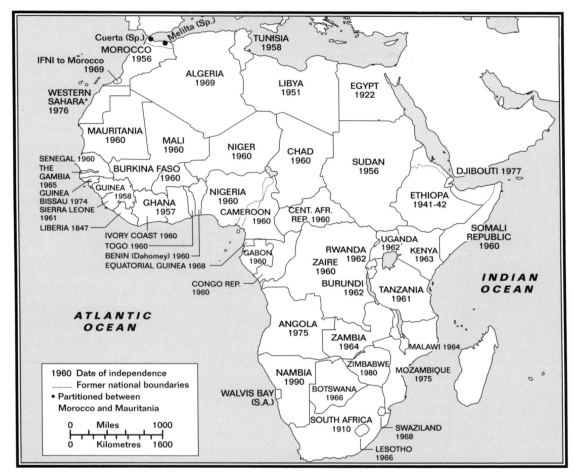

Cuerta (Sp.) · — Melilta (Sp.)

MOROCCO 1956
TUNISIA 1958
IFNI to Morocco 1969
ALGERIA 1969
LIBYA 1951
EGYPT 1922
WESTERN SAHARA* 1976
MAURITANIA 1960
MALI 1960
NIGER 1960
CHAD 1960
SUDAN 1956
DJIBOUTI 1977
SENEGAL 1960
THE GAMBIA 1965
BURKINA FASO 1960
GUINEA 1958
GUINEA BISSAU 1974
SIERRA LEONE 1961
GHANA 1957
NIGERIA 1960
CAMEROON 1960
CENT. AFR. REP. 1960
ETHIOPA 1941-42
SOMALI REPUBLIC 1960
LIBERIA 1847
IVORY COAST 1960
TOGO 1960
BENIN (Dahomey) 1960
EQUATORIAL GUINEA 1968
GABON 1960
ZAIRE 1960
RWANDA 1962
UGANDA 1962
KENYA 1963
CONGO REP. 1960
BURUNDI 1962
TANZANIA 1961
INDIAN OCEAN
ATLANTIC OCEAN
ANGOLA 1975
ZAMBIA 1964
MALAWI 1964
ZIMBABWE 1980
MOZAMBIQUE 1975
NAMBIA 1990
WALVIS BAY (S.A.)
BOTSWANA 1966
SOUTH AFRICA 1910
SWAZILAND 1968
LESOTHO 1966

1960 Date of independence
.... Former national boundaries
• Partitioned between Morocco and Mauritania

0   Miles   1000
0   Kilometres   1600

Nigerians proudly adopted a simply designed flag: a vertical band of white in the center, flanked by bands of bright green on each side. The white band signifies peace and unity. The green bands symbolize the country's long tradition of farming. Peace and unity, however, have eluded Nigerians, and its agriculture has faced severe challenges in the world market.

Africa after Independence, 1991

A CONTINENT OF NEW NATIONS

Independence was also spreading throughout the colonies ruled by France, Italy, and other European powers. The colonial era in Africa fast was drawing to a close.

Of all the evolving independent nations in Africa, Nigeria held perhaps the most promise during the early 1960s. Although greatly factionalized with its many geographic, cultural, and religious groups, it had achieved its independence in comparatively orderly fashion and seemed to be reasonably stable. It was a vast country with valuable natural resources. Increasing oil exports promised to bring it riches from the world marketplace.

As modern events have shown, however, long-term prosperity and stability were too much to expect of any emerging African nation. The new countries were thrust into a highly industrialized—and rapidly changing and growing—world economy. It was, all at once, both an exciting and frightening prospect.

All of western Africa since independence has been marked by a series of military takeovers, and Nigeria has been no exception. As in nearby countries, Nigeria has found it difficult to stabilize its economy to ensure orderly growth and development. The people's initial optimism and enthusiasm with the concept of independence have been replaced by confusion and disenchantment with the country's fragmented leadership.

A LOST LEGACY

One tragic result of European colonization is that it may have buried forever much that Africans had to offer the rest of the world. The Europeans succeeded in making Africans live and govern themselves more like Europeans. They took away many of the continent's physical riches to spread throughout the world. In the process they may have deprived the world of Africa's real treasures.

The early European visitors who explored and "developed" Africa devoted little time to chronicling the tribes and their histories. The Europeans were "in a hurry," as Richard E. Leakey writes: "In the basements of countless European museums, there are stacked shelves of African 'curios'—objects taken from the people but seldom documented in terms of the objects' use, customs, and history."

Cotton market at Bussa, 1898 *In 1898, Great Britain and France settled rival territorial claims in western Nigeria. France ceded some 31,000 square miles to the British, which included the town of Bussa. In 1900, the British recognized the Bussa chiefdom (founded 1730) as an emirate. Today, the emir functions in a traditional and religious capacity. The area is drained by several small streams that flow eastward to the Niger River. Poor soil and low rainfall have made this area one of Nigeria's poorest and least-populated regions. Gold mining, once important around Bussa, is no longer significant.*

To a great extent, Leakey believes, we have lost our chance to discover the continent's precolonial history. Africa, he says, "is a prime example of a continent where centuries of accumulated local knowledge is rapidly disappearing in the face of modernization."

This vanishing store of knowledge includes not just history but practical wisdom. One example, Leakey notes, is the

Inside Roof of Nupe House, c. 1900 *The Nupe people, who are farmers and craftspeople, live in west central Nigeria. They developed guilds for weavers, brass smiths, and other craft specialists. The Nupes are noted throughout Nigeria for their colorful glass beads, leather and mat work, brass trays, and fine cloth. Most Nupes are now Muslims but many older ceremonies are still performed. The indigenous religion included beliefs in a sky god and ancestral spirits.*

natives' use of wild plants for food and medicine. Generation after generation of tribal elders passed this information down. Today, such oral traditions don't seem as important either to the Africans or to outsiders. Modern-day Africans rely heavily on nutritional and medical knowledge and procedures taught to them by Westerners.

Leakey believes "the importance of new remedies based on age-old medicines cannot be underestimated. Over the past two decades, international companies have begun to take note and to exploit certain African plants for pharmacological preparations . . . which are, in most instances, nothing more than the refinement and improvement of traditional African medicine."

Leakey remains hopeful that "whilst it is late" to be recording details of traditional African use of wild plants for food and medicine, "it is not too late."

He observes, "It is indeed an irony that huge amounts of money are being spent by the advanced nations in an effort to discover life beyond our own planet, while at the same time nobody on this planet knows the extent and variety of life here at home. . . . [O]ne can only hope that Africa will become the focus of renewed efforts of research on biodiversity and tropical ecology."*

*See Dr. Leakey's introductory essay.

The Emir of Katsina, 1926 *The Hausa city of Katsina in northern Nigeria dates back to the 10th century. By the beginning of the 18th century, with a population of more than one hundred thousand, Katsina had become a major link in the trans-Saharan trade with Tripoli and Tunis. Kano was its principal rival. By 1750 Katsina had replaced Timbuktu as the chief West African center of Islamic studies. In 1903 British military forces conquered the city and forced the emir to pledge allegiance to the Crown.*

CHANGES DURING THE LAST 120 YEARS

Throughout history the struggle for independence has been a bloody undertaking for many nations (including the United States). For most African colonies, it required years of effort by nationalist-minded political groups. For some African countries, however, the actual change of power from foreign rule to home rule was comparatively nonviolent. Many former European government and military officials remained at their posts or were offered prominent positions in local politics and business. Most citizens noticed little difference in the way their country functioned immediately before and after independence day.

The world has been watching the newly independent nations closely. Statistics have been entered into economic, agricultural, sociological, medical, and other databanks, and the information has been disturbing. For example, many of the independent African countries are among the poorest nations in the world.

The reasons are many and complex. Most of the African countries had fairly sparse populations. Among other things, that meant that the native work forces and the native buying power could support few local industries. Besides cheap labor, industries required cheap energy sources. Saharan (northern) Africa is oil rich and comparatively wealthy; but throughout the rest of the continent, energy for factories was hard to

Ironworks, Near Lokoja, South Central Nigeria, c. 1912 *Nigeria has limited deposits of iron ore. The smelting of this ore stopped during the early years of British colonial rule. Since the 1960s, however, these deposits have been mined and shipped to the iron and steel complex at Ajaokuta in the lower Niger valley.*

come by. Coal—the primary source of energy for generations—was not plentiful, and hydroelectric (water-driven) power was expensive to develop.

Nigeria fared better than most of the other African nations. For one thing, it possessed substantial coal, natural gas, and iron resources. More importantly, it contained vast natural petroleum reserves. After years of probing, American and British oil com-

Warehouse, Kano, 1908 *By the 1820s the kingdom of Kano had become the major commercial power in West Africa. Its leather and cotton goods were transported northward by caravans across the Sahara to Fez, Tripoli, and Tunis—and then to Europe. However, by the 1880s, trade greatly diminished because of changing political conditions along the route and because of the arrival of Europeans on the West African coast.*

panies discovered oil of commercial proportion in 1956. They began exporting petroleum two years later. By 1980 Nigeria was pumping some 2 million gallons of oil daily. Along with Libya and Algeria to the north, it had become one of the world's leading oil suppliers. Approximately a third of Africa's petroleum reserves are believed to rest under Nigerian soil.

Agriculture, in contrast, faced problems all across the continent. Farmers were busy producing nonfood items like coffee and cocoa for export. As the continent's population began to multiply after World War II, many nations found they weren't growing enough staple crops to feed themselves. In addition, many individuals and families were moving from rural areas into the growing cities, where they believed they could earn more money and enjoy more modern conveniences.

The newly independent African countries had to borrow from other nations in order to provide for themselves. By the early 1980s Nigeria's foreign debt was estimated to be at least $10 billion. Problems mounted when world oil prices declined during the 1980s, posing a severe economic crisis for Nigeria.

LIFE IN NIGERIA TODAY

Daily life for people in Nigeria is much different from that of people in America. It's true certain similarities in lifestyle exist between citizens of Abuja or Lagos and residents of large American cities; and a few basic Western influences are strong (English, as we've seen, is the country's official language). If you went to live in Nigeria, however, you would have to get used to many shortages and inconveniences.

For instance, most of the travel (besides pedestrian and bicycle) is by bus. Only 1 in approximately 134 Nigerians owns a passenger vehicle of any kind. There are more scooters and motorcycles than private automobiles.

Earlier this century, railroads provided the primary means of travel and transport in Nigeria. But trains have fallen into disuse, partly because of dirty coach conditions, deteriorating service, and maddeningly slow speeds. Much of the country's railway system still uses outmoded narrow-gauge track, some a century old. A plan to replace it with modern, standard-gauge track in the 1980s was abandoned because of insufficient finances. This was followed by massive layoffs and strikes among rail workers.

Elephant Hunter, North Central Nigeria, c. 1900
Elephants, antelopes, hyenas, lions, and giraffes inhabit the tropical grassland area of north central Nigeria.

On average, there is only 1 television set for every 15 to 20 people. (Contrast that with the United States, where some homes have more television sets than residents.) Only 1 Nigerian in 5 (or 1 in 12, depending on the statistical source used) owns a radio. Many areas of Nigeria have no phones at all. According to estimates, there is 1 phone for about every 267 people nationwide. If you do have a telephone, don't expect problem-free service. "Nigeria's telephone system brings new meaning to the word 'awful,'" intoned one journalist.

There are frequent power outages and water shortages in some parts of the country. In the major port of Lagos, utility service is so unpredictable, according to a World Bank study, that half the industrial companies there (as of 1990) generated their own power supplies and almost two-thirds used their own well water rather than relying on municipal water service. Some operated their own phone systems.

Most workers in Nigeria, as in many other third-world countries, earn meager pay. Alarmingly, average individual incomes declined sharply during the 1980s, triggered by unfavorable oil prices. In the early 1990s Nigerian-born author Egbebelu Ugobelu calculated that whereas American factory workers earned more than $15 an hour, their Nigerian counterparts were earning as little as 12 cents an hour.

Opportunities are markedly fewer for Nigerian women than for men. In the north, as dictated by Muslim custom, many women marry in their early teens. Among certain farming cultures in various parts of the country, women are not permitted to work in the fields. Even among the wealthy, educated elite classes, many social functions are attended primarily by males. A national women's movement was organized in 1982 but was slow to gain public support.

The country's banking system, like its utility services, has a reputation for being unpredictable. At least part of the reason, reportedly, is that successive military governments often make changes to banking regulations. The nation's primary banking institution is the Central Bank of Nigeria. Some foreign banks have Nigerian branches, primarily controlled by Nigerian nationals. Nigeria's basic unit of currency (its counterpart to the American dollar) is called the *naira*.

Some Nigerians who live in the cities wear Euro-American clothing styles. Visitors to rural areas are more likely to see citizens dressed much like their ancestors. Light-colored, loose-fitting robes are worn by both men and women in some areas; many farmers wear only loincloths around their waists. Round caps are common headwear for men; scarves, for women.

If you sit down to dinner with a Nigerian family, you're likely to have corn, rice, yams, cassava roots, and a bananalike fruit called plantain. Hot pepper seasoning and palm oil are commonly used in cooking. Nigerians eat less meat than Americans; but fish, beef, chicken, and lamb are sometimes prepared.

The music, dance, art, and recreational forms seen today are in many ways similar to what the first Europeans discovered in the Niger delta. As with modern generations of every country, however, old ways have been fused with new ones, and modern entertainment vies for people's attention. Movie theaters can be

Egba Women Washing Clothes, Near Abeokuta, Southwestern Nigeria, c. 1883

Kanuri Wrestlers, 1904 *The Kanuri developed a powerful state in northeastern Nigeria. Kanuri society was divided into several distinct classes. Most, however, were commoners. The Kanuri were polygynous. The family unit lived in a walled compound of houses made from sun-dried mud bricks, which were either square or round, with flat or thatched roofs, respectively. Today, the Kanuri live in villages. They farm the sand soil of the surrounding countryside, with peanuts being the principal cash crop. Cowhide and goatskin are also exported in quantity.*

found in large Nigerian cities. Soccer is the country's most popular sport.

Marriages generally occur between couples of the same ethnic or religious community. Although mixed unions have become slightly more common in recent decades, marriages are still rare between, for instance, a Hausa-Fulani individual in the north and a partner from the southern or middle regions of the nation.

Nigeria's Principal Cities

As we have observed, although several other African countries are larger, Nigeria today has more citizens than any other African nation. Its population continues to grow. At the end of World War II, four Nigerian cities had more than 100,000 inhabitants each. Thirty years later, 32 of the nation's cities had exceeded the 100,000 mark.

Its capital city, Abuja, is located near the center of the country. It is not Nigeria's largest city. Abuja was designated the capital in 1991, succeeding the much larger port city of Lagos. Abuja was planned and developed in a beautiful, rolling valley. The planners' intent was to establish the capital in a location in which no single ethnic, social, or political group held control.

Highways connect Abuja to Nigeria's other major cities and towns in all directions. It's estimated that by the early 2000s more than a million people will live there.

Nigeria's other major cities include Lagos and Ibadan, each of which already has about a million and a half residents, at this writing. (By comparison, New York City—the most heavily populated city in America—has more than 7 million residents.) Lagos has an international airport, as does the city of Kano.

Lagos, an island city on the southwestern coast, is Nigeria's largest city and main seaport. Here, at the Nigerian Museum, visitors can examine the country's history, art, and ethnic distinctions. Portuguese mariners came to this area, which had been a settlement of the Yoruba people, in 1472, 20 years before Columbus's first voyage to the Americas. They named it Lagos after a port city in Portugal. Lagos later became an infamous slave trading center. Britain banned slave trading there when it annexed the territory in 1861.

Lagos was named the capital city by the British in 1914, when Nigeria was a colony. It continued to be the capital after Nigeria gained its independence in 1960, until Abuja replaced it.

Street Scene, Sokoto, Northwestern Nigeria, 1898 *Sokoto signed a commercial treaty with Great Britain in 1853. In the 1880s the people of Sokoto unsuccessfully opposed further British colonial expansion. In 1903 Britain conquered Sokoto and incorporated it into the protectorate of Northern Nigeria. Today, the Sokoto area is sparsely settled. The Fulani and the Hausa are the dominant ethnic groups. The majority of the population is Muslim.*

Other chief ports in Nigeria are Port Harcourt, Warri, and Calabar.

Much of the country's population is found not in large cities but in small villages, each with its aged headman, or chief. Nigerian houses range from modern to traditional structures. In coastal settlements you can see dwellings made with bamboo poles lashed together for the walls and broad palm leaves covering the roofs. In the interior woodlands and the upper savanna, many houses are made of mud and have grass-thatched roofs.

Government, Justice, and the Press

The country is divided into more than 30 states and a federal capital territory. In addition to its national government, it also has state governments—similar to the system of government in the United States. Military officials are in charge of the many smaller government jurisdictions found in each state.

Also as in the United States, Nigeria's constitution, drawn up in 1979, provides for a president. The constitutional system, however, has been violated with repeated military coups and presidential ousters.

Justice is meted out by both national and state courts. Over them all is a federal supreme court—again based on the United States judicial model. But the laws are not necessarily the same, either nationally or at lower court levels. Besides English law, the high court judges are versed in tribal customs of justice and in the laws of Islam.

Nigeria has a national police force, with a police inspector general appointed by the president. The organization has a reputation for being corrupt and inefficient, and its poorly paid police officers use outdated equipment. Much of the country's security rests in the hands of the military—an army of about 70,000 volunteers, augmented by a modest air force and navy.

Although Nigerian government has been unstable by U.S. and European standards and although most newspapers and broadcast media are owned by national or state governments, journalists in Nigeria are usually free to report what they observe. There have been cases of censorship, but these cases have not been as severe as in many countries where authoritarian governments virtually dictate what is "news" and what isn't. Nigeria also has several periodicals that are not directly under government control.

The typical Nigerian citizen may not share Americans' concept of freedom and the role of government in his or her life.

Courthouse, Kano, 1898 *By the 1820s the Hausa kingdom of Kano had become the greatest commercial power in West Africa and the major terminus for the trans-Sahara trade. In 1903 the British captured Kano and deposed the emir. This courthouse was located within the emir's compound, which was surrounded by the city's famous wall.*

The late Claude Ake, a Nigerian social scientist, observed that most residents of the sub-Sahara (that is, all of Africa south of the arid Sahara Desert region) are not as concerned with individuality (a vital characteristic to Westerners) as they are with their place in the community. Freedom, he explained, "is

Courthouse (left) and Prison (right) in the Kano Area, 1908 *After the British conquered Kano in 1903, they appointed the emir and all chief government officers. At first the British did not interfere with customary Islamic justice—as long as it did not contradict the laws of the British protectorate. However, no death sentence could be imposed without the approval of the chief British resident in Lagos.*

embedded in the realities of communal life; people worry less about their rights and how to secure them than finding their station and its duties and they see no freedom in mere individualism. Their sense of freedom is not . . . defined in terms of autonomy or opposition but rather in terms of cooperation and in the embeddedness of the individual in an organic whole."

ECONOMIC RESOURCES

Crude oil provides much of Nigeria's export economy. The United States and European countries are Nigeria's main trading partners. Also lucrative are the industries of mining, textiles, food processing, timber, rubber, and hides. About a sixth of the country is forested, but the modern timber industry has been hampered by illegal timbering practices.

Farming is the chief occupation of Nigerian workers, accounting for more than half the labor force. Cocoa is a major export crop. Still important today, as in colonial times, are palm products, rice, corn, cotton, and yams. About a third of the land is suitable for farming. Of the country's livestock, goats are most common. Cattle are raised primarily in the north.

Farming peoples often live in villages composed of family compounds. A *compound,* in this sense, is a collection of adjoining huts, each occupied by a related family.

Because of changing market prices and severe droughts, farm production has declined in the past thirty years. The nation's farmers are barely able to produce enough staple crops (such as corn and rice) to feed Nigeria's people. Nigeria, therefore, has to import basic foodstuffs.

This problem has worsened as a result of the dramatically increasing population. So many people from poorer neighboring countries immigrated to Nigeria that, during the mid-1980s, Nigeria closed its borders and deported more than a million immigrants.

Being a coastal nation with sizeable rivers running through its interior, Nigeria has always sustained an active fishing industry. Besides saltwater fishing in the Gulf of Guinea, fishers rely on freshwater rivers, creeks, and lakes, including Lake Chad more than 600 miles inland. Much of the fishing industry is based on small operations, using canoes and other light vessels.

Nigeria became increasingly industrial during the 20th century. Textiles are its chief manufacturing products. Compared to Europe and America, Nigerian industry is small and primitive.

Buduma Huts, Lake Chad, 1921 *The Buduma people, who are fishermen, live among the inaccessible islands and along the marshy northern shore of Lake Chad. They live in dwellings that vary from those made of straw to those built with hardened mud.*

In the late 20th century, Nigeria's economy was unstable. Compounding the difficulties just described has been the unpredictable oil market. When crude oil prices dropped in the early 1980s, the Nigerian government imposed austerity measures on the people and sought to diversify the economy. The most obvious solution was to expand agriculture; but farmers, as we've seen, had problems of their own.

EDUCATION

Formal education is not nearly as advanced in most African nations as it is in Western cultures. In Nigeria during the past century, schooling was provided through a combination of efforts on the part of the government, church groups, and native cultures. The type of school a young person attended depended largely on where the student lived.

Over the centuries Muslim cultures established Koranic schools in the north of Nigeria; education was part of Islam's religious requirements. Beginning in 1843, Christian missionaries introduced the first European schools in the southern part of the territory.

By the time the English colony was united in 1914, there were approximately 150 primary schools and 11 secondary schools in the southern region, run either by missionary organizations or by the colonial government. After World War II school attendance mushroomed across the land. According to estimates, primary schools in northern Nigeria were teaching 66,000 students in 1947; just 10 years later, the number was more than 200,000.

With independence, regional education budgets were increased. In the mid-1980s, the country had some 35,000 primary schools, with combined public enrollments of more than 13 million. Almost 4 million students were enrolled in more than 6,000 secondary schools.

Today, the Nigerian government provides free schooling from children six to fifteen years old. Although the government requires six years of primary education, about 40 percent of the people do not read or write.

After it became a nation, Nigeria established several universities. The country had 1,400 university students in 1960; in 1998 it had about 350,000. Teacher training and technical programs are important curricula.

Some Nigerian educators are frustrated that only a few of the nation's 37 universities have international reputations—which makes it difficult for Nigerian students to pursue further studies in foreign countries. A Nigerian history professor explained: "At one American university, the application form says if you are Nigerian and have not graduated from Ifè, Ibadan, or ABU, don't bother applying." University faculties in Nigeria have been cut dramatically.

In addition to classroom schooling, some young people learn different trades through apprentice systems. In return for training, the student works for the instructor for a specified number of years before becoming independent.

Medical Care

Health conditions are much worse in Nigeria than in better-developed countries. Basically, the country has one doctor per 5,000 people. There is not enough medicine to dispense to everyone who is sick.

Diseases such as malaria and yellow fever, which were conquered in America and Europe generations ago, still plague modern Nigeria. In recent years a meningitis epidemic took thousands of lives. A deadly, mysterious virus called Lassa fever, believed to be transmitted by rodents, took many lives. AIDS emerged as a major health threat during the early 1990s. Less serious diseases are numerous.

Health education and medical facilities have improved since independence, and vaccination programs have helped subdue some childhood diseases. There is, however, much to be done. Medical care is not available equally in all parts of the country or equally between the poor and the wealthy.

The average Nigerian lives only to about age 50. Approximately seven in 100 infants die in childbirth. In both lifespan and child mortality rates, Nigeria ranks in the bottom 15 percent among the countries of the world.

As with the schools, the first Westernized health care in the Niger area came with the missionaries. Roman Catholics in Abeokuta established the first hospital in 1860. One hundred years later, at the time of independence, Nigeria had more than 200 hospitals. Slightly more than half of them were missionary facilities; the others were government operated.

By the late 1970s the number of hospitals had almost tripled. Citizens were also served by almost 5,000 clinics, health centers, and maternity homes.

Modern Politics and Military Coups

If we were to refer to an almanac or encyclopedia to find out Nigeria's form of government today, we might find an answer such as "in transition." At first this seems to tell us nothing at all, but it actually reveals much about a changing, complex, often explosive part of the world.

Nigeria's first few years of independence were predictably rocky, as regional factions clamored for their share of power in the new representative government. Examples were the national census counts taken in 1962 and 1963. The population of a region determined how many seats it would have in the national house of representatives and the proportion of funds it would receive for government-sponsored projects. Stirred by local politicians, many citizens and census officials apparently cheated and manipulated the numbers in favor of their regions. After an initial tally showed a majority of citizens residing in the south, leaders in the north came up with approximately 9 million people who allegedly had not been included in the first report.

The country had many different political factions based in different regions when it became independent in 1960. A coalition of these regional parties formed the first independent government. But it fell apart in 1964, and law and order broke down in certain areas, particularly the west.

Still, Nigeria was considered one of the most stable democracies among the newly independent African nations. It even played a role in helping stabilize other, more volatile black nations. In 1964, for instance, Nigerian soldiers were at the core of a United Nations peacekeeping force sent to Zaire in Central Africa.

While nationalist political parties and leaders were coming to power in the independent African countries, military systems were also becoming powerful and sophisticated. The political leaders needed their armies in order to keep control. The military leaders, knowing this, became shrewd politicians in their own right. In situations in which they did not see eye to eye with the elected leaders, they began to take over their countries' governments. Some of these coups were accompanied by rioting and bloodshed; others were comparatively nonviolent.

In the past 30 years, Nigerian military and politics have played a strange power game. On more than one occasion, military regimes have banned all political parties in the country.

Public pressure ultimately forced the restoration of at least some of them, but the military continues to try to control them.

THE BIAFRAN DISASTER

The major political upheaval in Nigeria was both violent and catastrophic. Between 1967 and 1970, a major civil war caused more than a million deaths, either as a result of fighting or of rampant starvation and disease.

In a surprise coup army officers set up a military government under Major General John Aguiyi Ironsi in January 1966. The coup took place only days after Nigeria had hosted a British Commonwealth Conference—the first such conference ever convened outside England. The world had perceived Nigeria to be stable and progressive. Those who lived there knew otherwise.

The military takeover did not bring about a restoration of peace and calm among discontented Nigerians. Rather, it signaled the beginning of a frightening period of government intrigue. Within months Ironsi was killed in an army mutiny.

Another officer, General Yakubu Gowon, became Nigeria's leader. He succeeded in restoring order, but he could not stem the growing animosity between the residents of different parts of the nation. Tensions heightened between the Hausa and Ibo groups in the north. Thousands of Ibo were killed over a period of months; many others moved south to their ancestral tribal lands.

These events caused a national labor and transportation crisis. In a matter of days, for example, two-thirds of the laborers in the Jos Plateau tin mines left their jobs and homes. Also, Ibo workers had accounted for most of the railway force in the north.

During the spring and summer of 1967, General Emeka Odumegwu Ojukwu led the Ibo people in the east to declare independence from the rest of Nigeria. They called their new nation Biafra. They embraced independence ecstatically. Shops and businesses changed their names to reflect their Biafran identity. In one town journalists observed a newly mounted sign for the End of Nigeria Garage.

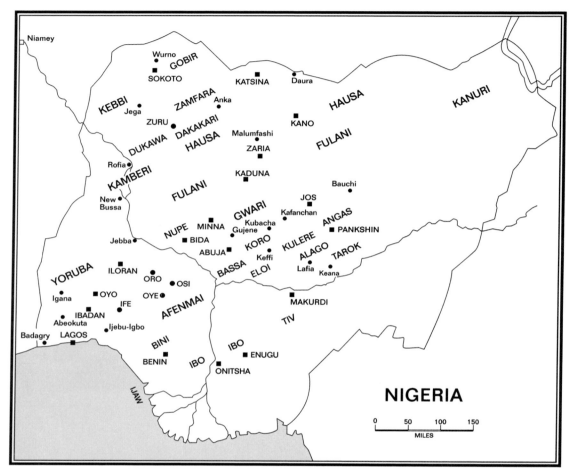

Niamey

Wurno
GOBIR
SOKOTO

KATSINA

Daura

KEBBI

ZAMFARA   Anka

HAUSA

KANURI

Jega
ZURU
DAKAKARI

DUKAWA   DAKAKARI
HAUSA

Malumfashi
ZARIA

KANO

FULANI

Rofia

KAMBERI

FULANI

KADUNA

Bauchi

JOS

Kafanchan

ANGAS

GWARI

Kubacha
Gujene

PANKSHIN

NUPE   MINNA

BIDA

KORO

KULERE

New
Bussa

Jebba

ABUJA

Keffi

ALAGO

TAROK

BASSA   ELOI   Lafia   Keana

YORUBA   ILORAN

ORO

OSI

Igana   OYO

OYE

IFE

AFENMAI

MAKURDI

IBADAN

Abeokuta

Ijebu-Igbo

TIV

Badagry   LAGOS

BINI

IBO

IBO

BENIN   IBO   ENUGU

IJAW

ONITSHA

NIGERIA

0   50   100   150
MILES

Names and locations of traditional tribes

Independence euphoria was short-lived, however. In the war between the Biafrans and Gowon's army that followed, both sides carried out bloody massacres. They brought in mercenary airmen—some of them bomber and fighter pilots, others gun-runners—and commando leaders and units, veterans of the legendary French Foreign Legion, and other armies. Civilians lived in terror.

Within a year the Biafran nation was on the decline. Deadly military opposition from Nigeria, a ruined economy, and internal dissent deprived the new nation of any real chance of success. Nnamdi Azikiwe, perhaps Nigeria's most prominent founding father, initially favored a separate Biafra, but in 1969 he changed sides. He urged the Ibo people to abandon their leader, General Ojukwu.

It was the first large-scale civil war to be covered by television-based media. The world was appalled by images of the dead and wounded and by the fact that the victims and their enemies ironically held so much in common—only a few years before, they had together celebrated independence from English rule.

The emaciated bodies of the hungry haunted the viewers, who were secure in their own homes and societies. The world learned that there are two kinds of starvation: *marasmus*, in which the human body shrinks to skin and bones because of the lack of food, and *kwashiorkor*, in which protein deficiency leaves the victim with a bloated stomach but spindly arms and neck—(the result of the body literally cannibalizing itself). Apart from the fighting, *kwashiorkor* is believed to have caused most of the deaths during the Biafran struggle. Relief supplies and workers were sent from different parts of the world.

In the end the Biafrans surrendered. In January 1970 the union was restored and Ojukwu had to flee. Gone was the End of Nigeria Garage. Instead, news photos showed a smiling Nigerian youth at a rally holding a hand-painted sign: "OBITUARY. BIAFRA IS DEAD. AGE 2 YEARS." Nigeria was a united nation once again—but at an astonishing cost.

Power Plays and Corruption

Upheavals have become an accepted part of Nigerian life. After one episode of postelection violence in 1966, a government newspaper headline proclaimed with something of a sigh of relief: "*Only* 153 People Killed in the West."

Since then the country has been embroiled in repeated struggles between elected leaders and military strongmen. In 1979 an elected administration brought democracy to Nigeria after 13 straight years of military control. Four years later, however, the government was overthrown. Two years after that, General Ibrahim Babangida seized power.

In 1993 Babangida authorized another presidential ballot; but he threw out the election of Moshood Abiola, declaring the voting results illegal. After months of bloody riots, Babangida was replaced briefly by a civilian leader, who in turn was replaced by another military regime. When Abiola boldly declared himself president of the country, based on the election returns, he was thrown in jail.

After General Sani Abacha took power in 1993, he established a hard brand of authority. "Any attempt to test our will will be decisively dealt with," he proclaimed. Abacha dismissed local elected officials and banned political parties. He later withdrew the political ban, but unrest during his reign was often violent; more than a hundred people were killed by police in one riot. Abacha died in 1998. His successor was another military strongman, General Abdulsalam Abubakar.

The internal power struggle for Nigeria has at times been quiet but frequently bloody. Opposing factions resort to brutality and terrorism. Politicians like Abiola know they might be jailed. Beko Ransome-Kuti, a leading prodemocracy activist, has been imprisoned many times. Some, like environmentalist and playwright Ken Saro-Wiwa, have been executed. Saro-Wiwa was hanged by Abacha's officers in 1995. His death angered the international community; many countries imposed sanctions against Nigeria.

Clashes between religious factions, sometimes tragic, have also continued into the 1990s. The varying interests of these groups are woven into the fabric of national politics. Nigerian internal disputes are difficult for the country's own leaders to untangle and are almost impossible for outside observers to understand fully.

Stress in Daily Life

Besides political and religious violence, Nigeria has languished in disturbing ways under enforced military rule. Everyday business and financial transactions are uncertain. The quality of higher education reportedly has declined.

Unemployment became a national crisis during the 1970s. Part of the problem was the migration of thousands of farm workers to the cities, where they hoped to find better-paying jobs. Thousands of students were dropping out of school and entering the work force—which could not support such numbers. Unemployment was especially high in the eastern Ibo region.

This dilemma was worsening during a period when the north of Nigeria and adjoining countries underwent one of the worst agricultural droughts of the century. Famine took many lives in neighboring nations, and refugees flocked to Nigeria. Meanwhile, growing native populations in areas like that of the Ibo in the southeast hastened depletion of the farmland.

Part of the Nigerian merchant community, after centuries of earning wide-ranging respect for their trading enterprise and wisdom, have turned to drug trafficking to make their fortunes. Although Nigeria is not a major producer of illegal drugs, it has become known among international law enforcement agencies for its drug-running syndicates. Some whole villages reportedly are involved. During the 1980s, approximately 15,000 Nigerian nationals were arrested around the world for transporting and dealing in drugs.

Observers fear the problem is worsening. A United States Drug Enforcement Agency official in 1995 declared that Nigerian heroin syndicates are pivotal in illegal international distribution of that substance.

The ineptness and corruption of the country's government officials have made their way into business and industry. One example in 1975 caused a domino effect of problems. That year found the port of Lagos jammed with hundreds of cargo vessels. Their crews waited many months for permission to unload. More than 200 of the ships carried cement to be used for public roads and buildings.

During the harbor crisis, unscrupulous merchants and middlemen mixed spoiled cement with good cement in order to sell it. After it eventually was used in construction projects, the roads eroded easily in heavy rains. Relatively new buildings began to collapse.

A Human Tragedy

As in other countries where such political and economic corruption exist, the ordinary people suffer most. Individuals and families who have little and who struggle just to survive find themselves homeless and caught between opposing forces.

The Biafran calamity was a sobering lesson for Nigerians of every faction. The human and economic toll was felt by everyone. Since then, the government has moved quickly to put down large-scale ethnic unrest and to protect the basic rights of minorities. (Local government officials in the north reportedly preserved the properties of Ibo citizens who fled that region during the civil war, and afterward returned the properties to them.) Nigerian leaders fear not just the awesome costs of civil violence but the world's reaction to it.

Still, ethnic strain is one of Nigeria's most unsettling concerns. This is especially true in the cities and regions where many ethnic groups with longstanding differences live and work together. Ethnic jokes and other prejudices are common.

In some regions ethnic majorities control hiring practices—most notably for local government jobs. In certain situations ethnic bonding is considered more important than trade unions for securing favorable conditions among work forces. Observers note that riots by unorganized farmers and trade laborers seem almost as likely to occur as organized strikes by unions.

At the beginning of the 21st century, Nigeria is viewed by many as a nation held in limbo by its military leadership. In 1960, when it became independent, it was seen as a model for other African nations as they cast off colonial rule. Now it is regarded with despair, even embarrassment.

Could the Problems Have Been Avoided?

A 1991 report by the U.S. Federal Research Division to the Library of Congress listed some of the events and pressure points that have come to bear on Nigeria in the last century: "the imposition of colonial rule, independence, interethnic and interregional competition or even violence, military coups, a civil war, an oil boom that had government and individuals spending recklessly and often with corrupt intentions, droughts, and a debt crisis that led to a drastic recession and lowered standards of living. Under such circumstances, people tended to cleave to what they knew. That is to say, they adhered to regional loyalties, ethnicity, kin, and to patron–client relations that protected them in an unstable and insecure environment."

Journalist Karl Maier, in his book *Into the House of the Ancestors*, writes that in today's Nigeria, it seems that "everything is possible, yet nothing is possible." The country produces brilliant writers, musicians, athletes, and artists. "It is also a land whose people race around furiously just to stay in the same place, not to lose ground to the rising waves of poverty, of dirt, of despair about the future of their children. All the while, a tiny wealthy elite hovers around a sumptuous banquet set by a clique of military officers with unbridled access to the fruits of Nigeria's multi-billion-dollar oil-exporting industry."

Richard E. Leakey has pointed out that African history "has been presented from an entirely Eurocentric or even Caucasocentric perspective." That is, we're taught mostly what Westerners in Africa have discovered and done themselves during the past five or six centuries.

"The time has come," Leakey suggests, "to regard African history in terms of what has happened in Africa itself, rather than simply in terms of what non-African individuals did when they first traveled to the continent."

CHRONOLOGY

A.D. 1000   European merchant seamen have begun exploring and trading along the western and eastern coasts of Africa. Meanwhile, Africans in the northern coastal territories are now trading across the Sahara Desert with other natives in the lower interior. Most African peoples have shifted from hunter-gatherer livelihoods to farming.

1086   The Kanem-Bornu people in the region of Lake Chad (bordered by what are today Nigeria, Niger, Chad, and Cameroon) adopt Islam as their religion.

Circa 1400–1800   Europeans establish regular trade along the lower coast of West Africa, including what is today coastal Nigeria. The Niger River region becomes the primary outlet for the transatlantic slave trade.

Late 1700s   Protestant societies in Europe begin to send missionaries to West Africa. Catholic leaders, in turn, expand their own African mission work, begun centuries earlier.

1792   Denmark becomes the first European country to abolish its slave trade. England follows in 1807 and soon deploys a naval blockade off the West African coast to intercept slave ships.

1817   Usuman dan Fodio dies. His Sokoto Caliphate—the largest kingdom on the African continent—is divided.

1820–30   The great Oyo Kingdom west of the Niger splinters into small states.

1861   Britain establishes a colony at the port of Lagos.

1877   Englishman George Goldie makes his first exploration of the Nigerian interior.

1884–85   European leaders discuss their interests in specific African territories at the West Africa Conference, held in Berlin. Some historians contend that the great European powers in effect "partitioned" Africa at the conference.

1886   The British government charters the Royal Niger Company for trading.

1899   Frederick Lugard is appointed high commissioner of Britain's Nigerian territory. He sometimes uses force to bring natives under English dominion.

1914   Great Britain unifies its northern and southern "protectorates" in the Nigerian basin. Lagos is named the colony's capital city.

1920s   A growing spirit of nationalism begins to take root in Nigeria.

1925   The British government initiates improvements in the mission schools of the Niger basin.

1956   American and British oil companies discover vast oil reserves in Nigeria.

CHRONOLOGY

1957	Ghana, a former British colony west of Nigeria, becomes independent.
1960	Nigeria becomes independent after a three-year transition period.
1964	Nigeria's initial coalition government breaks down, beginning a thirty-six-year succession of military takeovers and failed attempts at elected leadership.
1967–70	The Ibo people in eastern Nigeria declare their independence as the nation of Biafra. More than a million people die in the ensuing civil war. Biafra ultimately is defeated and the region is reunited with Nigeria.
1979	Nigeria formulates its national constitution—but many of its fundamental precepts continue to be violated.
1980s	World oil prices decline, triggering a serious, long-standing economic crisis in Nigeria.
1991	Abuja becomes Nigeria's capital city.
1998	General Abdulsalam Abubakar, another military strongman, becomes Nigeria's head of state.
1999	Several years of military rule come to an end when the country successfully holds democratic elections. Olusegun Obasanjo wins 63% of the vote and becomes the president

ONE SUMMER'S DAY in 1830, a group of Englishmen met in London and decided to start a learned society to promote "that most important and entertaining branch of knowledge—Geography," and the Royal Geographical Society (RGS) was born.

The society was formed by the Raleigh Travellers' Club, an exclusive dining club, whose members met over exotic meals to swap tales of their travels. Members included Lord Broughton, who had travelled with the poet Byron, and John Barrow, who had worked in the iron foundries of Liverpool before becoming a force in the British Admiralty.

From the start, the Royal Geographical Society led the world in exploration, acting as patron and inspiration for the great expeditions to Africa, the Poles, and the Northwest Passage, that elusive sea connection between the Atlantic and Pacific. In the scramble to map the world, the society embodied the spirit of the age: that English exploration was a form of benign conquest.

The society's gold medal awards for feats of exploration read like a Who's Who of famous explorers, among them David Livingstone, for his 1855 explorations in Africa; the American explorer Robert Peary, for his 1898 discovery of the "northern termination of the Greenland ice"; Captain Robert Scott, the first Englishman to reach the South Pole, in 1912; and on and on.

Today the society's headquarters, housed in a red-brick Victorian lodge in South Kensington, still has the effect of a gentleman's club, with courteous staff, polished wood floors, and fine paintings.

WORLD WITHOUT END

The building archives the world's most important collection of private exploration papers, maps, documents, and artefacts. Among the RGS's treasures are the hats Livingstone and Henry Morton Stanley wore at their famous meeting ("Dr. Livingstone, I presume?") at Ujiji in 1871, and the chair the dying Livingstone was carried on during his final days in Zambia. The collection also includes models of expedition ships, paintings, dug-out canoes, polar equipment, and Charles Darwin's pocket sextant.

The library's 500,000 images cover the great moments of exploration. Here is Edmund Hillary's shot of Sherpa Tenzing standing on Everest. Here is Captain Lawrence Oates, who deliberately walked out of his tent in a blizzard to his death because his illness threatened to delay Captain Scott's party. Here, too is the American Museum of Natural History's 1920 expedition across the Gobi Desert in dusty convoy (the first to drive motorised vehicles across a desert).

The day I visited, curator Francis Herbert was trying to find maps for five different groups of adventurers at the same time from the largest private map collection in the world. Among the 900,000 items are maps dating to 1482 and ones showing the geology of the moon and thickness of ice in Antarctica, star atlases, and "secret" topographic maps from the former Soviet Union.

The mountaineer John Hunt pitched a type of base camp in a room at the RGS when he organised the 1953 Everest expedition that put Hillary and Tenzing on top of the world. "The society was my base, and source of my encouragement," said the late Lord Hunt, who noted that the nature of that work is different today from what it was when he was the society's president from 1976 to 1980. "When I was involved, there was still a lot of genuine territorial exploration to be done. Now, virtually every important corner—of the land surface, at any rate—has been discovered, and exploration has become more a matter of detail, filling in the big picture."

The RGS has shifted from filling in blanks on maps to providing a lead for the new kind of exploration, under the banner of geography: "I see exploration not so much as a question of 'what' and 'where' anymore, but 'why' and 'how': How does the earth work, the environment function, and how do we manage our resources sustainably?" says the society's director, Dr. Rita Gardner. "Our role today is to answer such questions at the senior level of scientific research," Gardner continues, "through our big, multidisciplinary expeditions, through the smaller expeditions we support and encourage, and by advancing the subject of geography, advising governments, and encouraging wider public understanding. Geography is the subject of the 21st century because it embraces everything—peoples, cultures, landscapes, environments—and pulls them all together."

The society occupies a unique position in world-class exploration. To be invited to speak at the RGS is still regarded as an accolade, the ultimate seal of approval of Swan, who in 1989 became the first person to walk to both the North and South Poles, and who says, "The hairs still stand on the back of my neck when I think about the first time I spoke at the RGS. It was the greatest honour."

The RGS set Swan on the path of his career as an explorer, assisting him with a 1979 expedition retracing Scott's journey to the South Pole. "I was a Mr. Nobody, trying to raise seven million dollars, and getting nowhere," says Swan. "The RGS didn't tell me I was mad—they gave me access to Scott's private papers. From those, I found fifty sponsors who had supported Scott, and persuaded them to fund me. On the basis of a photograph I found of one of his chaps sitting on a box of 'Shell Spirit,' I got Shell to sponsor the fuel for my ship."

The name "Royal Geographical Society" continues to open doors. Although the society's actual membership—some 12,600 "fellows," as they are called—is small, the organisation offers an incomparable network of people, experience, and expertise. This is seen in the work of the Expeditionary Advisory Centre. The EAC was established in 1980 to provide a focus for would-be explorers. If you want to know how to raise sponsorship, handle snakes safely, or find a mechanic for your trip across the Sahara, the EAC can help. Based in Lord Hunt's old Everest office, the EAC funds some 50 small expeditions a year and offers practical training and advice to hundreds more. Its safety tips range from the pragmatic—"In subzero temperatures, metal spectacle frames can cause frostbite (as can earrings and nose-rings)"—to the unnerving—"Remember: A decapitated snake head can still bite."

The EAC is unique, since it is the only centre in the world that helps small-team, low-budget expeditions, thus keeping the amateur—in the best sense of the word—tradition of exploration alive.

"The U.K. still sends out more small expeditions per capita than any other country," says Dr. John Hemming, director of the RGS from 1975 to 1996. During his tenure, Hemming witnessed the growth in exploration-travel. "In the 1960s we'd be dealing with 30 to 40 expeditions a year. By 1997 it was 120, but the quality hadn't gone down—it had gone up. It's a boom time for exploration, and the RGS is right at the heart of it."

While the EAC helps adventure-travellers, it concentrates its funding on scientific field research projects, mostly at the university level. Current projects range from studying the effect of the pet trade on Madagscar's chameleons, to mapping uncharted terrain in the south Ecuadorian cloud forest. Jen Hurst is a typical "graduate" of the EAC. With two fellow Oxford students, she received EAC technical training, support, and a $2,000 grant to do biological surveys in the Kyabobo Range, a new national park in Ghana.

"The RGS's criteria for funding are very strict," says Hurst. "They put you through a real grilling, once you've made your application. They're very tough on safety, and very keen on working alongside people from the host country. The first thing they wanted to be sure of was whether we would involve local students. They're the leaders of good practice in the research field."

When Hurst and her colleagues returned from Ghana in 1994, they presented a case study of their work at an EAC seminar. Their talk prompted a $15,000 award from the BP oil company for them to set up a registered charity, the Kyabobo Conservation Project, to ensure that work in the park continues, and that followup ideas for community-based conservation, social, and education projects are developed. "It's been a great experience, and crucial to the careers we hope to make in environmental work," says Hurst. "And it all started through the RGS."

The RGS is rich in prestige but it is not particularly wealthy in financial terms. Compared to the National Geographic Society in the U.S., the RGS is a pauper. However, bolstered by sponsorship from such companies as British Airways and Discovery Channel Europe, the RGS remains one of Britain's largest organisers of geographical field research overseas.

The ten major projects the society has undertaken over the last 20 or so years have spanned the world, from Pakistan and Oman to Brunei and Australia. The scope is large—hundreds of people are currently working in the field and the emphasis is multidisciplinary, with the aim to break down traditional barriers, not only among the different strands of science but also among nations. This is exploration as The Big Picture, preparing blueprints for governments around the globe to work on. For example, the 1977 Mulu (Sarawak) expedition to Borneo was credited with kick-starting the international concern for tropical rain forests.

The society's three current projects include water and soil erosion studies in Nepal, sustainable land use in Jordan, and a study of the Mascarene Plateau in the western Indian Ocean, to develop ideas on how best to conserve ocean resources in the future.

Projects adhere to a strict code of procedure. "The society works only at the invitation of host governments and in close co-operation with local people," explains Winser. "The findings are published in the host countries first, so they can get the benefit. Ours are long-term projects, looking at processes and trends, adding to the sum of existing knowledge, which is what exploration is about."

Exploration has never been more fashionable in England. More people are travelling adventurously on their own account, and the RGS's increasingly younger membership (the average age has dropped in the last 20 years from over 45 to the early 30s) is exploration-literate and able to make the fine distinctions between adventure / extreme / expedition / scientific travel.

Rebecca Stephens, who in 1993 became the first British woman to summit Everest, says she "pops along on Monday evenings to listen to the lectures." These occasions are sociable, informal affairs, where people find themselves talking to such luminaries as explorer Sir Wilfred Thesiger, who attended Haile Selassie's coronation in Ethiopia in 1930, or David Puttnam, who produced the film *Chariots of Fire* and is a vice president of the RGS. Shortly before his death, Lord Hunt was spotted in deep conversation with the singer George Michael.

Summing up the society's enduring appeal, Shane Winser says, "The Royal Geographical Society is synonymous with exploration, which is seen as something brave and exciting. In a sometimes dull, depressing world, the Royal Geographical Society offers a spirit of adventure people are always attracted to."

FURTHER READING

de St. Jorre, John. *The Brothers' War: Biafra and Nigeria.* Boston: Houghton Mifflin, 1972.

Encarta 98 Encyclopedia.

Encyclopaedia Britannica (*Micropaedia* and *Macropaedia* volumes), 1995.

Hargreaves, J. D. *Decolonization in Africa.* Essex, England: Longman Group, UK Limited, 1990.

Koslow, Philip. *Centuries of Greatness: The West African Kingdoms.* New York: Chelsea House, 1995.

Lamb, David. *The Africans.* New York: Random House, 1982.

Maier, Karl. *Into the House of the Ancestors: Inside the New Africa.* New York: 1998.

Metz, Helen Chapin, Ed. *Nigeria: A Country Study.* Washington D.C.: Federal Research Division, Library of Congress, 1992.

Oliver, Roland, and Fage, J. D. *A Short History of Africa*, 6th ed. New York: Facts On File, Inc., 1988.

Pakenham, Thomas. *The Scramble for Africa: The White Man's Conquest of the Dark Continent from 1876 to 1912.* New York: Random House, 1991.

Rowell, Trevor. *The Scramble for Africa (c. 1870–1914).* London: B. T. Batsford Ltd., 1986.

Ugobelu, Egbebelu. *Divided We Die: Bulls-Eye Solution to the Cyclical World Recession and Nigeria's Socio-Economic Problem.* Charlotte, N.C.: Obiesili Publishing, 1994.

Wesseling, H. L. *Divide and Rule: The Partition of Africa, 1880–1914.* Westport, Conn. Praeger, 1996.

World Almanac & Book of Facts, 1997.

World Book Encyclopedia, 1999.

An excellent website for life in contemporary Nigeria is Governments on the WWW.Nigeria {http://www.gksoft.com/govt/en/ng.html}. Follow the hyperlinks for additional information on this country.

ABOUT THE AUTHORS

Dr. Richard E. Leakey is a distinguished paleo-anthropologist and conservationist. He is chairman of the Wildlife Clubs of Kenya Association and the Foundation for the Research into the Origins of Man. He presented the BBC-TV series *The Making of Mankind* (1981) and wrote the accompanying book. His other publications include *People of the Lake* (1979) and *One Life* (1984). Richard Leakey, along with his famous parents, Louis and Mary, was named by *Time* magazine as one of the greatest minds of the twentieth century.

Daniel E. Harmon is an editor and writer living in Spartanburg, South Carolina. The author of several books on history, he has contributed historical and cultural articles to *The New York Times, Music Journal, Nautilus,* and many other periodicals. He is the managing editor of *Sandlapper: The Magazine of South Carolina* and editor of *The Lawyer's PC* newsletter.

Deirdre Shields is the author of many articles dealing with contemporary life in Great Britain. Her essays have appeared in *The Times, The Daily Telegraph, Harpers & Queen*, and *The Field.*

INDEX

Numerals in italics indicate a photograph of the subject mentioned.

INDEX

INDEX

INDEX

INDEX

INDEX